Ideas and Ideologies
General Editor:
Eugene Kamenka

Law and Society

The Crisis in Legal Ideals

**Edited by Eugene Kamenka,
Robert Brown
and Alice Erh-Soon Tay**

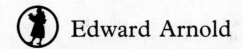 Edward Arnold

© Edward Arnold (Publishers) Ltd 1978

.First Published 1978 by
Edward Arnold [Publishers] Ltd
25 Hill Street. London WIX 8LL

Law and society. – (Ideas and ideologies).
  1. Sociological jurisprudence – Congresses
  I. Kamenka, Eugene   II. Brown, Robert
  III. Tay, Alice Erh-Soon   IV. Series
  340.1'15   [Law]

  ISBN 0–7131–5994–4
  ISBN 0–7131–5993–2   Pbk

Filmset and printed in Great Britain by
Willmer Brothers Limited, Birkenhead

Contents

Introduction

'Ideas and Ideologies', as a series of studies in the history of ideas, includes what might be called the history of contemporary ideas, It aims to connect the past, the present and the future, the 'material' and the 'intellectual', the social and the personal. It will seek to study and exhibit ideas and ideologies in their theoretical complexity but to see them at the same time as both agents and products of those social changes that have helped to shape the modern period. It will be especially interested in ideas or concepts that themselves function as ideology, that are history- and theory-laden and embody the striving to change the world by, and while, re-describing it.

In pursuing this aim the series will present monographs and collections of essays by able and distinguished thinkers. Their studies, on the whole, will move across the boundaries of particular disciplines as narrowly conceived and bring men, ideas and specific disciplinary problems into relation with each other and set them in a wider cultural context. *Law and Society, Bureaucracy, Imperialism, Human Rights* – to mention the volumes now completed or in preparation – indicate, even by their titles, the combination of range and critical bite that this series hopes to achieve.

The historian of ideas must look to the present and the future as well as the past if he is to be a judge and critic of human endeavour and not just a worthy antiquarian. Only thus can he be more than a recorder of bygone fashions, no matter how transitory or insignificant, a *voyeur* immersed in the spectacle for its own sake, a relativist with no yardstick of his own. If his discipline is to aspire, as I believe it should, towards a fundamental assessment of man and a total critique of culture, then it needs a concept of great traditions, of abiding problems and of their interaction with overpowering events. It requires a concept of classical periods, of culture and civilization, of the human predicament and of world-historical forces and demands, a sense of centre and periphery, foreground and background, as well as an appreciation of that which is, at various times, overpoweringly *novel* in human affairs. Such concepts provide no substitute for detailed knowledge and 'feel', no recipe for neatly trimming the epochs of history, no guarantee that certain factors will always reveal themselves as central or significant and others as peripheral or derivative. Nor are such concepts properly to be stereotyped into rigid, simplistic criteria of cultural 'success' or 'failure', 'worthiness' or 'unworthiness'. But only such concepts can make us recognize the past, the present and the future as part of one story and enable us to understand and to judge each of them in the light of the others. The capacity to do that is the difference between culture and provincialism, between sustained and responsible critical thought on the one hand, and the related extremes of empty 'tolerance', abstract moralism, unstable enthusiasm for fashion or 'relevance' and the rigid unthinking adherence to tradition and 'standards' on the other. In the serious and ambitious study of ideas in their historical development and context, thinking in the humanities and thinking in the social sciences become closely intertwined, illuminating each other and creating a unified cultural tradition and a literary-historico-philosophical capacity for understanding. It is to the furtherance of such a tradition and of such understanding that this series is, in the eyes of its editor, committed.

Certain modern or post-modern trends, which provide the background to this opening volume, have tended strongly in the opposite direction—towards rejecting the concept of culture, civilization and classical periods, towards pitting 'humanity' or 'democracy' or 'equality' against history and complexity, tradition and institutions, towards elevating the individual against everything that stands outside him and elevating the demands of the present against everything that has come before. Such low-level 'consciousness' *uses* the past as an enormous museum, as a random collection of bric-a-brac, from which it believes it can draw items at will, abstracting them from their social and historical context and from the particular kinds of men and women who created them. This technique has impoverished our lives while it appears, superficially, to enrich them; it has made us become *actors* in the bad sense that the word had for the Romans— people capable of assuming any personality because they have none of their own.

The historian of ideas who values truth and accuracy, let alone his own reputation, will not venture lightly into describing a historical period as *the* age of anything; he will not treat any society as displaying a set of coherent, consistent and pervasive attitudes; he will know from experience that the day's revolution always began at least one hundred years earlier and that future ages will be struck, often above all, by the continuities that persist through 'revolutionary' change. In any case, he will have no doubt that what the revolutionaries achieve will be very different from what they wanted to achieve and that their rhetoric does more to conceal than to illuminate some of the most important changes that are taking place.

Granting all this, one cannot deny that the last decade has witnessed a dramatic shift in the public tone and style of social, cultural and political life. As always, the new attitudes that come to the fore have an earlier, 'underground' history; as always, there are earlier historical periods, previously held in contempt, which suddenly serve to justify and remind us of our own. Each revolution writes its own prehistory and begins by seeking to show that the orthodoxy it wants to overthrow was a time-bound, non-universal, aberrant condition of the human race. At the moment there are many—none of them, I would think, of the first rank as thinkers—who are engaged in doing that for almost the whole of the Western culture. There has thus been a (temporary?) retreat, from the mature Karl Marx whose thinking ushered in so many of the themes of modern life, to Ludwig Feuerbach. There has been a shift from science and *Realpolitik* to primitive Christianity, love-mongering and astrology; from Marx's version of a law-governed world, in which factors of production produce occupations and classes and occupations and classes produce men, to anthropotheism, the elevation of man in general and his (or her) abstract rights and requirements. Marx's emphasis on objectivity and thought has given way, in many circles, to the primacy of feeling and will. We have turned from the social elevation of those who do to the social elevation of those who suffer (an elevation that once provided the ground for the primary socialist objection to Christianity, that it was a religion that had no conception of production).

There is, in consequence, something that might be described as a contemporary crisis in law, justice and morals in Western post-industrial societies—the appearance of an unusually strong and widespread revulsion from the style, attitudes, presuppositions and arrangements implied in the ideal of a society governed by laws and not by men and made up of specific men, institutions and provinces rather than abstract individuals. It is with aspects of that crisis, in its bearing on law and society, that this volume attempts to deal. The contributors trace the conflict through contemporary legal philosophies and perceptions of law, through socialism and liberalism, the concepts of property, rights and welfare, criminology and penology in order to gain a serious understanding of the modern condition. In doing so, they return constantly, in the context of the development of modern culture and of their own disciplines and interests, to themes that must be of concern to all men and women today—the relationship between freedom, determinism and responsibility, between the role ascribed to the individual and the different ways of conceiving society, between the emphasis on legal, moral and cultural traditions and sensitivity to oppression, inequality and the 'hell of bourgeois existence'.

The idea of this volume, and the papers collected within it, arose out of a three-day seminar arranged in Canberra in August 1975 by the three editors on behalf of the History of Ideas Unit in the Research School of Social Sciences of the Australian National University and the Department of Jurisprudence in the Faculty of Law of the University of Sydney. That seminar, on the theme 'A Revolution in our Age? The Transformation of Law, Justice and Morals', was attended by historians, philosophers, political scientists, social theorists, lawyers and students of literature; it considered some thirty papers, a number of which have provided the nucleus for further titles in this series.

The editors of this volume would like to express their gratitude to members of that seminar, to Mrs V. Wetselaar, Mrs D. Mitchell and Miss M. O'Neill for the typing and preparation of the manuscripts, to Mrs E. Y. Short for checking the manuscripts and proofs and preparing the index and to Edward Arnold and its editors for the encouragement and care that they, too, have lavished upon this book and the series it is intended to inaugurate. I am also grateful to the Editor of the *Dalhousie Law Journal* for permitting Professor Morison to publish in this volume a revised and expanded version of an article first written for, and published in, that journal and to the Max-Planck-Institut für ausländisches und internationales Privatrecht in Hamburg for giving me facilities, in September 1976, to work on this volume and others in the series.

Canberra, March 1977   Eugene Kamenka

I

Law, the citizen
and the state

Alice Erh-Soon Tay

I

There is, in many quarters today, a remarkable hostility to law, as a social institution, as an intellectual discipline and as a repository of values. Some of this hostility is associated with the bursting forth of a *Lumpenbourgeoisie* and a *Lumpenintelligentsia*, seeking support and inspiration from that external proletariat which stands on the fringes of industrial and post-industrial civilization and sees, to the exclusion of all else, its own needs and deprivation, demanding instant recognition and satisfaction. More of it rests on the increasing social concern with, and visibility of, a new kind of internal 'proletariat', the materially, educationally, intellectually deprived who need and demand state protection rather than the opportunity to exercise their rights, who—wrongly—see past and existing law as always helping someone else. The radical shifts in the relationship between the law, the citizen and the state which these developments are producing, the consequent assault on classical conceptions of the individual, of freedom and responsibility, are to some extent masked by the continued and indeed ever-increasing but crucially new use of the word 'rights'—as in women's rights (to state- or employer-subsidized crêches, for instance, free abortion or wages for rearing children). The distinction, of course, is the distinction between 'freedom from' and 'freedom to'. When F. D. Roosevelt proclaimed as part of the allied war aims the right to 'freedom from want' and 'freedom from fear', he was proclaiming not an immunity but the foundation of the welfare state; he was guaranteeing a claim upon the organized machinery of society for the material preconditions of freedom and personality and calling these guaranteed claims 'freedoms' in their own right.

The contributions that these guarantees and the development of the welfare state have made to the alleviation of all sorts of human miseries are enormous and the need for such contributions is obviously not exhausted. The danger does not lie in helping the poor, the weak, the sick, the incompetent. It does not lie in the principle of taking from those who have in order to alleviate the condition of those who have not. The danger lies, as it always does, in elevating one social problem above all others on the plea of urgency; it lies in making all social institutions, all education, all moral attitudes part of a crude and blatant social machinery for achieving one aim—an aim that is necessarily, in these conditions, unsubtly conceived, shorn of its complexities, simplified and vulgarized to such a degree that simplification and vulgarization become characteristics of the whole society.

The machinery of administration, let alone that of law, is by contrast subtle and complex and the very people who believe that it should be operating at full steam for the speedy realization of the common good flee from its disturbing complexities, just as they flee from the disturbing complexities of real individuals, concrete rights and conflicting social claims and demands. We live in an age no longer of real individualism, if only for some, but of pseudo-individualism for all. Never in public life have people been more willing to talk about themselves, to see their own egos as the centre of the universe and the true end of civilization; never have they been less perceptive, and less honest, about themselves and their problems. They want to touch others, to have encounters, because they cannot bear to live with themselves. It is precisely this emotional and intellectual dishonesty that forms the real content of the attack on objectivity and the demand for 'commitment' or 'communication'— the demand that the facts be not allowed to stand in the way, that the medium itself become the message, that content take second, third and ultimately no place. It is one thing to recognize that there are occasions in human history, for example, in the civil rights movement in the United States in the late 1950s and early 1960s, when a demonstration has to be made, when initial action must precede discussion and analysis of the consequences because the evil is monstrous and manifest. It is another thing to erect a general philosophy on this foundation, to elevate the abstract moral act over the thought-out programme, individual feelings over social consequences, one's own problems over everybody else's. To have that type of philosophy one has to have a certain type of mind, at once shallow and dangerous, strident and insensitive, simple and self-righteous—a kind of mind that a surprising number of schools and universities, teachers and counsellors, are busy producing today in the name of self-expression. This is what I call pseudo-individualism— emotion without competence and without that self-assurance which is grounded in knowledge and capacity and experience, self-importance without the readiness to take responsibility, longing without staying-power, social and intellectual pretension without the habit of sustained planning and sustained work.

People, even politicians and political activists—perhaps especially politicians and political activists—tend to think in black and white and they tend to think of one thing at a time. To reduce all problems to one problem is to give oneself the comforting illusion that the crisis is manageable, that the future can be shaped by a single act of will and that the consequences of our actions can be predicted easily; it is to believe that a new society can be built, almost overnight, to a plan as one demolishes a building and erects a new one. It is this which is implied in our current devaluation of institutions, constitutions, traditions, limited functions and experts and expertise—unless, in the case of the latter, they happen to be committed to our goals and ready to provide instant legislation that claims it will achieve them.

We have created a whole new language devoted to nurturing and promoting this illusion, a language that talks about 'the system' instead of people and institutions, about 'restructuring' instead of changing, about 'consciousness' and 'consciousness-raising' instead of history and development, about (abstract) 'confrontation' instead of 'crisis', with its implication of concern for a wider whole—a language, in short, that pretends that history is bunk, that context is irrelevant and that the individual will is omnipotent or at least ought to be. When reality proves us wrong, we drop out, like the child that refuses to talk to its playmates. It is not surprising that it is a language taken up most enthusiastically by the men and women of the media, by those who exercise, in the most manifest way, power without responsibility. The two institutions that have shaped my life and whose values I would want to go on shaping my life—the law and the university—stand for precisely the opposite morality, for a sustained and critical examination of the facts, for a constant regard for consequences, for a belief in the capacities, creativity and moral value of the *historical* human spirit operating in a social context, for a recognition of the worth, fragility and complexity of human association and the intricate set of economic, social, moral and cultural ties on which it rests. There is a curious notion abroad that the law and the concern with cultural and intellectual values are by their nature rigid, divisive, obstacles to progress and change. This seems to me nonsense. Nobody who has studied the history of the common law in England and in the English-speaking world can fail to marvel at the way it has been shaped to take into account and to facilitate change, to enable men to do, in an orderly and responsible way, what has never been done before. Lawyers, especially unintelligent lawyers, may be rigid: the law is not. Capitalism was born in England, out of a feudal society which it turned topsy-turvy. There the whole field of land law, through that remarkable institution the trust, was revolutionized to make that transition possible, a whole new area of commercial law and company law was developed, great judges, much more than legislators, saw the realities arising around them and the potentialities inherent in the common law for dealing with the affairs of men even as they change their character. No one who has studied literature or history or law can believe, for one moment, that these stand for the immutability of men, societies, or human affairs—that *change* was discovered, or promoted, for the first time in 1968, or by one's favourite, and most recent, social democratic or revolutionary government. On the other hand, one has only to compare the totally ideological, legally meaningless, bills of rights incorporated in the French constitutions with the powerful and significant first ten amendments to the United States constitution to understand the emptiness of rights not grounded upon and protected by developed legal traditions and institutions, precedents, case-law and a genuinely independent judiciary.

II

Today, changes as momentous as those that overtook eighteenth- and nineteenth-century Britain are overtaking the whole world, sweeping through the whole area of social life, requiring new social, legal, administrative and political developments but requiring, above all, thought that will bring them into relation with each other, that will see how complex and intricate the revolution in our lives is proving to be and that will enable us to see and to plan where we are going. Talk about community, for example, may express the very real fear of atomization and loneliness and powerlessness produced by individualism in the conditions of a modern, economically competitive, but state-controlled, mass society; but it also masks the fact that almost every demand made by those who speak in the name of community is a demand for further extending the already momentous social role and growing claim to moral responsibility of the state and its administration. The revolution in our law is not a revolution substituting organic togetherness and community values for the commercial-individualistic model of law which reached its apogee in the attitudes of both nineteenth-century German Civilians and common lawyers like Dicey; it is a revolution replacing contract between the parties by contract dictated from above, law by administration, politics by ombudsmen, property by hand-outs, individual legal responsibility by statistical analyses and consequent 'treatment' or manipulation.

Most of these shifts, I believe, are to an important extent inevitable and irresistible: if nineteenth-century liberalism as a coherent philosophy providing the basis of law and government is collapsing, this is because reality has seriously outstripped and undermined it, has turned many of its assumptions into fictions so patent that they no longer have real social reference or social bite. We cannot meet the present by simply clinging to the shibboleths of the past; thinking cannot come to a halt, cannot rest on its laurels, cannot say, there I have done my work and my truth will stand for all time.

Nevertheless, I still do not believe in the integration (for which read *Gleichschaltung*) of the university and the law into the general machinery allegedly working for the common good. 'A university', as Professor Kamenka has written, 'is neither a microcosm of society nor a temple of youth. A university as an institution is concerned with and embodies a *particular* social interest—the interest in truth as a condition of culture, of rationality and rational action, of technical competence and social and intellectual judgement. A university, as an institution, is thus concerned with promoting the *discipline* of enquiry, the *intellectual organization* of knowledge, the *rigour* of argument and the *drawing of distinctions* between the true and the false, the good and the bad, the relevant and the irrelevant, the competent and the incompetent.' Law stands on the same morality, coupled with the knowledge that it must live with what it creates. Both see the individual, not as an empty, abstract, puffed-up ego crying 'Give!' and entitled to be satisfied, but as a complex economy of motives, attitudes and capacities for action, all of them to be *judged* in the context of their bearing on his relationship with others, in the light of the actions they issue in, the consequences they lead to.

A world in crisis, a society in change and confusion, needs such concerns far more than it needs cultist pseudo-individualism, whether promoted through trendy politics, trendy education, trendy media, trendy churches or 'consciousness-raising' slogans devoted, unthoughtfully, to promoting a shallow concern with the here and now. Instant individuals and instant solutions, like instant coffee and instant soups, will not do. What resists change at all costs, on the other hand, is not always or even overwhelmingly conservatism or self-interest, it is as often unintelligence and ignorance. The task of education and thought is to save us from unintelligence and ignorance on the one hand and from its mirror image, empty utopianism and sloganizing, shallow 'trendiness' and flight from responsibility and intractability on the other. These two sides, indeed, promote each other. Today's trendies, or the effective ones among them, are tomorrow's authoritarians. Freedom involves protest and a sense of the worth of the concrete, not abstract, individual, that is, it involves critical thought, moral courage and social and intellectual responsibility.

The retreat from culture, which is also the retreat from concrete, sustained, self-developing and responsible individualism, is evinced in our constant focusing on the physical and material preconditions of the spiritual life, whether of the individual or of the society. A naive sociology and a naive social psychology, uncritical, ahistorical, abstract and abstracting, readily degenerating into the so-called science of communication, have replaced history, philosophy, literature and law as the great moulders of mankind. Of course, this shift of interest has helped to cure some of the blindness of the past—to bring to our sympathetic attention what it is fashionable today to call the disadvantaged and the underprivileged and to give us a much better understanding of their problems and concerns. But where the movements of the deprived and oppressed themselves are fundamentally educative and formative movements, movements in which one learns discipline, understanding, responsibility, sustained effort, competence and skill through the fight against hardship and oppression, the concept of the disadvantaged is one that involves a belief in their present sub-humanity, in their fundamental dependence on benefits brought them by others. The dependence of the men, women or groups that require hand-outs is not genuinely overcome by announcing that they have a right to such hand-outs, that they are receiving not charity but their alleged due as human beings. They are still receiving. Coupled with the currently fashionable egalitarianism, the insistence that we are all fundamentally of the same character, worth and potentiality, this leads—from the side of the state—not to the self-sovereignty of the underprivileged and deprived, but to the ultimate dependence of every citizen. It is still in work, in creating or doing competently, rather than in receiving, that men and women find their dignity and worth; it is the extension of enterprise and of the capacity for enterprise that is the ultimate test of freedom.

What, then is the basis of genuine and concrete individualism for which state benefits and material facilities can only provide a precondition, but to which they cannot give direction and content? The real basis, it seems to me, is what was traditionally meant by culture before the word was debased—those social, moral and intellectual traditions, and their requisite material foundations, that make it possible to cultivate the individual, nurture him in a social setting, give him character in the moral sense of the word, a character that includes understanding, responsibility towards oneself and others and compassion. The political expression of that culture, with which genuine individualism is intimately bound up, is not the state but law, law not as the arbitrary will of the sovereign, or as a great inchoate flood of legislative acts 'reforming' this and that, but law as a live and continuing tradition, based on a belief in justice and maximum individual sovereignty, on a recognition of the complexity and conflict involved in human affairs, and on the internalization of the principal norms of that tradition by the vast majority of the population as part of their language and their culture. That is the Western idea of law, born in

Rome, but perfected, I still believe, in the common law rather than the far more state-centred, bureaucratized, codified legal systems which most of continental Europe derived more directly from the Roman law.

The life of the common law, the life that has made it a charter of liberty *against* kings, barons, prelates, oligarchs, ministers, bureaucrats and tyrannous and intolerant majorities, cannot be summed up in a few abstract principles. The very essence of the common law, as a charter of liberties, has lain in its constant, meticulous concern with the matter before the court, with real people and real social situations, whose problems were not analysed for cost-benefit by the state to show that they were not worth the trouble. The great European legal systems of private law are all based on an adjudicative conception of law that implies the equality and equivalence of abstract juridical subjects, individuals, as bearers of rights and owers of duties; these systems therefore strive toward and reach their conceptual perfection in the *Gesellschaft* which sees the state as just another party to a relevant contract including the social contract. But the common law is a *Gesellschaft* system firmly rooted in a *Gemeinschaft* setting, socially, stylistically and, in part, conceptually. The civil law of the Continent and of most of the socialist-communist countries is also a *Gesellschaft* system, but it is firmly rooted in and controlled by bureaucratic-administrative structures and conceptions. That is one of the important contrasts between a case-law system and a code: logically, they operate in much the same way, but *psychologically*, the case system constantly invites the detailed consideration of particulars, and of people, as part of a specific *real* situation. Common law, unlike Bentham and the civil law, recognizes no hypothetical paradigms, no abstract invented code or textbook illustrations of a principle; it looks to real cases as historical events, arising in an actual social, psychological and historical setting, incorporating *dialogue* between counsel and the judges, between the judges on the bench, and between the judges and their predecessors who live, as people, in the cases they have decided. It is only in common law reports that the parties have names, histories, personal quirks and come to life through the description of a total social situation. In the French reports, they are characterless; they appear as instances, or objects, of a general rule, and what is worse, they do so, according to the French, in their own interest, to preserve their anonymity.

Beneath this habit or style lie three principles fundamental to Western law and Western civilization, without which, I believe, genuine concrete individualism cannot survive. The first is the independence, the formal procedural impartiality and comparative predictability, the rule-governed nature, of the law and its courts. This implies the existence of law as a system and of lawyers who have been trained to understand and cherish it and to feel their own behaviour to be bound by it. If modern tribunals, which are at best quasi-courts, have not yet in English-speaking lands reverted to being star chambers, this is because, and only because, the common law and its procedures have entered into our souls and still govern what is accepable and what is not.

At least some of the current hostility to law is based on the belief that this elevation of an impartial, rule-bound, conflict-resolution-oriented judiciary interferes with social planning and social reform, that it protects existing and entrenched interests against the requirements of the future, of the rational allocation of necessarily limited resources, that it focuses too much on the past and the parties and never on the whole or the common social interest. Law, it is argued, should give way to social 'science' and political policy, courts to commissions, precedents to statistics, and judges to economists or to those who see as their primary function the implementing of socially or politically determined goals—that is, to the politically committed or those willing to serve. Plan, as the Soviet legal theorist E. B. Pashukanis believed, should replace law, principles of socialist upbuilding, socio-economic norms, should be substituted for the civil code and the norms of civil law relations, concepts of social harm and social danger should do, more efficiently, the work of such antiquated, individualist concepts as civil wrong and criminal offence, as fault and *mens rea*.

The conflict is a conflict of two paradigms, neither of which has ever been put into effect in pure, unmitigated form, and either of which would by itself lead to appalling results. But there is, in too many quarters today, a willingness to move from the obvious need for application of the new paradigm in certain areas to a total willingness to destroy the old and this willingness is indeed leading to new forms of star chamber, to tribunals and so-called courts (like some of the new family courts) that become a scandalous law unto themselves precisely because of their informal or mixed procedures, because they are exposed neither to public scrutiny nor to the full rigour of proper judicial appeal and because they have before them, in too many cases, second-rate lawyers. There is no doubt that we must, in modern society, greatly extend the range of non-judicial, quasi-judicial and administrative commissions and tribunals in ways which, both in principle and in practice, have always been perfectly familiar to the common law and have rested on a proper recognition of its limitations. But to use the need for such commissions and tribunals to destroy the social acceptance of, and respect for, those principles of judicial impartiality and independence and of rule-governed behaviour by which the common law and the common lawyer live is to court disaster.

Another attack on the principle of judicial impartiality, independence and consequent remoteness and technicality comes not from the elevation of resource allocation, but from the romantic yearning for fireside equity. This is the desire for the informal 'human' resolution of conflict in a *Gemeinschaft* as opposed to a *Gesellschaft* manner, that is, by *ad hoc*, flexible justice or by ritualized procedures that emphasize reconciliation, enabling the parties to live together, rather than sharpening the point at issue and then deciding it without fear or favour. It is, of course, true that the *Gesellschaft* has always been and should always be humanized by *Gemeinschaften*, that people constantly resolve disputes outside the framework of formal justice. It is a pathetic commentary on the atomization of modern society, on the sheer 'lostness' of so many modern men and women, that they should look to the state and its formal machinery to provide the human element in their lives, the neighbourly relations, the feeling of belonging to a community. The state is neither competent to assume that role as part of its judicial and administrative function, nor to be trusted within it.

Social distance is unpopular today and judges are often seen and criticized as remote, class-bound, removed from real life, geared to middle-class values. Of course, there have been and are judges who are narrow-minded, unimaginative, prejudiced and, much more frequently, senile, just as there are politicians and administrators who are these things. It is easy to underrate the enormous experience of life at all levels, the sense of social difference and social complexity, that lies at the very heart of law and that good barristers and judges acquire and strengthen, day after day, as a direct result of their work. Both social reformers and politicians and most administrators have seemed to me in these matters far more untutored, imperceptive and remote than good solicitors, barristers and judges. The elevation of the politician as the principal law-maker (and law-breaker) of modern life is far from being an unmixed blessing.

The second principle fundamental to our law and civilization is the principle of the abstract equality, equivalence and imputed moral freedom and responsibility of the parties. For the purposes of both civil and criminal responsibility, common law treats men and women as adults, as possessed of free will, the capacity to choose and the resultant responsibility for their actions. The belief in free will may be a myth; it is certainly, in the law itself, a defeasible presumption. It is also, quite properly, restrained in its effects by reference to ancillary circumstances, by the plea in mitigation, by the new concept of diminished responsibility, by a host of subsidiary concepts that allow play for other factors. But in a society which simply rejects this fiction and treats all people before it as patients to be cured and not as agents to be judged, I would not care to live. It would turn our whole world into a gigantic mental hospital in which the doctors would be the law, and in which each individual doctor, as in Stalin's Russia and Mao's China, would himself be a potential patient.

The perniciousness of destroying notions of personal responsibility is, on the whole, widely recognized in the area of criminal law, except by those, like the new criminologists discussed in Dr Brown's article, who want to treat crime as simply a manifestation of the class war. It is not accepted anywhere near so widely in the field of tort and civil law generally, where actuarial considerations of cost-benefit through universal social insurance and a growing belief that people must be protected at all costs from their own stupidity, incompetence and gullibility hold far greater sway and raise much more complex problems. These problems still need to be discussed and analysed, carefully and conscientiously, rather than swept aside in the rush toward the 'progressive'.

The third principle that has been fundamental to Western law and especially to common law has been the notion of an area of personal inviolability, reflected in the fact that the action for trespass, whether to the person or his land, was the first and most important action at common law, rooted in an even older Anglo-Saxon and Norse concept of seisin that stands at the very centre of the development of democracy in northwestern Europe. It is a concept intimately connected with, almost indistinguishable from, the often derided centrality of property in the law. Property is that which a man has a right to use and enjoy without interference; it is what makes him as a person and guarantees his independence and security. It includes his person, his name, his reputation, his chattels, the land that he owns and works, the house he builds and lives in and so on. These things are seen as his property in early law because they are seen as the reification of his will, as the tangible, physical manifestation of his work and his personality.

Common law, in formulating a concept of property, departed in one very significant way from the Roman tradition which still dominates continental Europe. In Roman law a man's right to use and enjoy, to the exclusion of others, flowed from title, from a state-recognized acquisition or transfer of ownership. In common law, already looking to the facts rather than authority, ownership flowed from possession, from actual use and enjoyment, no matter how acquired. The Roman lawyer, forced to recognize, as one must, the possible bifurcation of enjoyment and the right to enjoy, was satisfied to look to the question of right. He derived title from previous title and recognized rights flowing from physical possession or enjoyment only in so far as such possession or enjoyment could be treated as a (deficient) form of ownership, of the assertion of a right. The Roman lawyer, in short, was a natural bureaucrat. The early English lawyer, on the other hand, looked primarily to the possession or enjoyment itself and saw rights as flowing from it. The assize of novel disseìsin, the assize of mort d'ancestor and the other special assizes that followed all recognized only one ultimate way of establishing a right to enjoy—that is to show that you or your ancestor had enjoyed before the defendant or his ancestor and that your enjoyment was taken away unlawfully and without your consent, or before you had time to take seisin as heir. So strong was the refusal to treat a right as something abstract, incorporeal and detachable from physical fact, that even rights other than the right to enjoy (advowson, freedom from toll, for instance) could be established at law only by showing that they had been exercised and enjoyed. It is precisely because the concept of seisin is *not* founded on right that the thief himself can have seisin; it is because all proprietary and possessory rights ultimately stem from enjoyment that seisin lies at the very root of the development of the English law of property and of the Englishman's concept of freedom—of his home as his castle.

The common law, then, begins with and long maintains a bias in favour of the factual situation—the citizen's actual behaviour and powers *against* the claims of privilege and authority as such. Certainly, there must have been some tension between what one might call the politically democratic concept of seisin and the importance in feudal society of acquiring grants or enfeoffments from feudal superiors. There is little doubt that the charter of a great baron and the charter, word or deed of the king successfully put an end to rival claims. But the interesting point is that such feudal acts do not seem to become part of the common law as a system; they rather suspend legal process, putting an end to litigation by the authority of power. Even later, when the law of real property had come to recognize rights existing independently of enjoyment, the inferiority of 'seisin in deed' to 'seisin in fact' shows the continuing weakness of right *sans* enjoyment within the law.

Both economic life and the common law have undergone enormous change since the concept of seisin stood explicitly at the centre of our law. Ownership and control no longer part company as an exception; in the commercial world indicia of title have become infinitely more important than chattels and even in ordinary life men no longer simply own, let alone make, what they use. Nevertheless, the recognition of the not uncommon link between property, possession and enjoyment —the paradigm of property personally used and controlled—should not be given up lightly. Commercial developments over the last four hundred years, and political and administrative developments over the last hundred years, have made this no longer the most important and socially visible type of property. However, the coming of the affluent society in the West and more recently in socialist-communist countries has greatly increased the number of people who have such significant 'personal' property and who look to the law to protect and safeguard their highly intimate and personal use and enjoyment of it. This is why communist theorists now stress that Marx and Engels never meant to abolish private property in the sense of property for personal use and enjoyment; instead, it is claimed, they meant only to abolish private property in the means of production, distribution and exchange, that is, property as the source of unearned income or as power over others to direct, manage and 'exploit' labour. The role of the underlying seisin-possession concept in the common law is to recognize and protect those still important areas in which men live, work and plan as users-owners, to set out their rights and obligations, to give them an area of privacy in which they have a right to be free of state and community interference, to repel the unattractive neighbour, the busybody, the officious policeman, and to ensure that they allow their neighbours the same possibility of undisturbed enjoyment. Only in societies that do not have such protection do men realize how important this concept of personal security and inviolability is. It is the alleged Maoist contempt for such social and human rights that has formed, for the past ten years, the gravamen of Soviet theoretical attacks on social conditions in the People's Republic of China, an attack which the ordinary Russian, through his experiences under Stalin, instantly understands and applauds. It is also the base and shaper of the social sentiment that shrinks with distaste from the forcible eviction.

The fundamental social importance of the abstract legal concept of property—the power to use, control and dispose of, to the exclusion of others—is made evident to us by the fact that this concept as such has not changed, in abstract definition, since Roman times, though all the powers implied in the concept may be limited by the intervention of legally sanctioned authority, as they have always been. This is why the concept of property continues to play a central role in the legal systems of all socialist and communist governments. As control or the right to control, it provides in both communist and Western systems of law the nexus for most tortious/delictual obligations and for a wide range of obligations to the state, to planning authorities and under welfare or social-protective norms. The civil codes of the USSR, as Soviet theorists themselves stress, are based on the fundamental civil law relation of debtor and creditor and the planning systems of both the USSR and the People's Republic of China are organized on that basis, in other words, on the existence of civil law relations and definable property boundaries between productive units and enterprises.

The abstract concept of property as the legal recognition of a partly infra-jural fact, or of the legal necessity to make somebody ultimately responsible for the control and disposal of a thing, is not at stake in any modern society. The problem, which arises quite early in Western law, is that of the divorce which may occur between possession as actual control, as a matter of fact, and ownership as the ultimate but unexercised or delegated right to control, based on title. In certain types of property, the divorce between these two aspects of ownership/possession has become increasingly the norm. This fact does not invite us to alter the classical definitions of ownership and possession, which remain as they were, but rather to distinguish different types of property as giving rise to different problems in the exercise and protection, or limitation, of ownership and control. This happens, of course, because in concrete conditions different types of property have different social effects. This in fact is precisely the distinction made by all modern legal systems and state regulations. They control not property as such, by altering the whole concept; they regulate for, or against, specific types of property such as private housing, industrial estates, public companies. They regulate for them in different ways and in different connections, as much in communist countries as in 'capitalist' countries. In doing so, the legal systems of these societies have passed very markedly from a predominantly *Gesellschaft*, conflict-resolution concern with disputes between property owners, including the state as a property owner, to a bureaucratic-administrative, regulatory and even confiscatory resources-allocation concern, in which the state stands above property owners, as the representative of a general 'socio-political' interest. The focus in social regulation and resources allocations is on *activities*, on the *use* made of property and its effect on other people, other activities, the national economy and the availability of resources. Such regulations, for all their piecemeal and *ad hoc* character, do tend to build up into a body of law governing a whole social province or function—economic law, the law of broadcasting, of fisheries, of urban construction and development, of agriculture, and of welfare and social insurance. This is why both common and code law countries have been enacting or discussing quite new kinds of codes—economic law, law regulating securities and investments,—providing for new types of offences that are 'economic' or 'administrative' rather than directly criminal or delictual.

Professor C. B. Macpherson[1], in an important plea for a new extended definition of property that would return to what he takes to be a precapitalist notion of common property and of property as a right to a revenue, is not concerned with the present situation of property at all, or with its present role in the legal system. He is interested in certain socio-political rights (rights to protection or benefits through state regulation) being given the kind of social imprimatur and ideological status that property enjoyed for a limited period in the

---

[1] C. B. Macpherson, 'Capitalism and the Changing Concept of Property' in Eugene Kamenka and R. S. Neale (eds), *Feudalism, Capitalism and Beyond* (London and Canberra, 1975), pp. 104–24.

recent history of Western Europe, when the property owner in principle confronted the state as an equal, if not a superior. Behind this there may be a further assumption that would create a more genuine link with the concept of property—the conception that all property, both state and private, is socially and not individually created, that the state and, perhaps, the large corporation hold property only *in trust* and that the citizens therefore have a claim on such property, at least a claim to participate in its management, to share in its use, to receive some of its benefits. This is, in a sense, a genuine demand for the socialization of property, limited, one suspects, to the property of the state and large corporations and institutions, not applicable to the corner grocer shop, my neighbour's house or the small agricultural holding. The demand, of course, is not an attempt at competing legal interpretation; it is a radical political demand for the socialization of large-scale property and social institutions. For the lawyer, the striking thing about that is that access, participation and benefits still have to be apportioned out, made the subject of defined and allocated individual rights. Instead of being property rights under common law, they would have to become status rights under a system of administrative regulation, such as are represented and reified by readers' tickets to the British Museum, social insurance cards and labour exchange registration numbers. This is what Roscoe Pound meant when he wrote in 1930 that, having moved from status to contract, we were now moving back to status, to a new feudalism in which the state was the grantor of benefits.

In a very influential article[2], Professor Charles Reich saw claims of this type, based on our special or general status as citizens, employees, aborigines, as the new wealth that the individual has in the collective society. He argued that such claims must be made inviolate against the arbitrariness of the state and the tyranny of majorities in the way in which the legal status accorded the concept of property sought to make man's wealth inviolate in a previous age. But Reich's plea, in the final sentence of the article, that we must create a new property is merely a rhetorical flourish. Unlike Macpherson, he is not looking to private law and its concepts at all; rather he wants a new homestead act for twentieth-century man, that is, an administrative enactment that will protect man's new rights and requirements, but protect them with the same fervour as law in the past has protected man's (private) property.

For a point of departure, I stand closer to Reich than to Macpherson. I do not believe that the new developments in the control and regulation of property and the new status and administrative demands which citizens make on bases other than property can or need be systematized within the tradition of the common law or the concepts of private law by attempting to write them into the definition

[2] Charles Reich, 'The New Property', (1964) 73 *Yale Law Journal*, p. 733.

of the concept of property, though I do believe that the concept of property as such cannot be and must not be excised from the law. The rights linked to the traditional concept of property have always been defeasible and men have always had claims and rights not based on property. It would be odd to elevate property into a ubiquitous concept at the very time that its social role and importance are being seriously diminished. On the property side, as I have suggested, the task is to distinguish, in terms of their social implications and effects, between different types of property (consumption property, production property, for instance) for the purpose of framing specific and appropriate legislation and regulation. This, as I have also argued, is precisely what has been happening. On the other claims that citizens are now making—claims for access to and a voice in the control of publicly significant institutions, the right to employment, social and economic security, and so on,—it seems to me best to treat such claims as what they are, claims to social rights, or more accurately benefits, not derived from property. This is why the non-property-based rights guaranteed by the US constitution and its amendments have come to play such an important role in the recent history of that country; this is why the proclamation of a bill of rights has support not only in the UN but even in Australia, where reliance on the common law as the protector of liberties against the state has been strong. But without the common law or a comparable judicial tradition to serve as a matrix, such declarations and bills of rights become, as they have been in France ever since 1792, nothing but pious and legally inoperative pieces of ideologizing. In the recognition of these rights, however, as in property rights, we have to distinguish, in terms of their concrete social implications, between different rights and thus recognize that the method of their implementation and the defeasibility or non-defeasibility of the claim may vary. Men may and now do seek abstract guarantees of the satisfaction of these rights, but they look in respect of most of these rights to the resources and the allocative machinery of the state for practical implementation. We thus have what appears at first sight to be a traditional legal conception of rights coupled with an explicit or implicit demand for administrative-regulatory machinery on which the citizen can rely to provide satisfaction of those rights. Macpherson emphasizes the possibility of grounding such new claims in private law concepts; Reich and the many US lawyers who have followed him, as befits citizens of a country in which the constitution can convert almost all private law into public law, emphasize the administrative-regulatory side; they seek to ground claims in public law, to demand a direct state guarantee of benefits, or of largess and, in some areas, to impose on the state a doctrine of public trust. All avoid the central fact, that the distinction is no longer between private and public law, or crudely between 'private' and 'public' interest; it is between an adjudicative system of justice and an administrative one. It is quite clear that the body of administrative regulation hitherto recognized and acknowledged by the common law as statute or statute-based can no longer be dealt with entirely within the confines of the common law. It will develop into a distinct body of law and legal arrangements, striving towards some internal coherence and external generality, inviting codification, the creation of even more special tribunals and a whole system of administrative justice, bringing separate tribunals into relation with each other and with a general concept of administrative procedure and review. One of the things that this will involve will be the cutting down, both legally and practically, of areas of administrative discretion; it will, in short, arouse and respond to a concept of administrative rights parallel to, and in many ways now at first sight more important than, what Englishmen used to call their common law rights. These latter will persist in some areas of social life; they will be less and less directly important in others, where the administrative rights will become central. But if that centrality becomes more than a centrality within the system of administration, if it comes to dominate our language, our culture and our social life, we will be so much the poorer.

There is, then, no point in simply and simplistically looking backward to a society in which property and property-based rights occupied a position of overwhelming social and legal centrality—no merit in attempting to deal with new developments on the model of even a fundamental concept of private law. The need now is to consider, as a problem of both justifying and properly limiting state intervention, the social and economic effects of particular types of property and to set out and explore these distinctions and the difffering provisions they require in a body of administrative regulation. There is also need to consider and define the non-property-based rights that our society, or, more accurately, our government, is willing to recognize, satisfy and protect, to distinguish those necessarily or best dealt with through the regulatory or administrative machinery of the state and to legislate for them in enactments which, like factory and social insurance legislation, are clearly not derived from the common law. To advocate this is not to suggest that these codes will be the pure work of reason, gifts of an impartial and omniscient lawgiver and planner who creates his systems *de novo*. The claims he recognizes will be actual historical claims; the future he envisages will be grounded in the present. His law, at this level more than at any others, will be politics.

The real, fundamental 'philosophical' question that should dominate the discussion of law, politics and society today is how to define and to shape the character, procedures and spirit of such a new system of administrative regulation and, in the final event, of administrative justice. The investigative tribunal, the informal court, the ombudsmen, the mixed administrative and judicial bodies created under many laws dealing with areas or activities—for example, the land and valuation court, the bankruptcy court, the new family courts, the various bodies provided for administrative review and appeal— have given us some history to go by and they have, in modern conditions, also reacted back on the common law, whose judicial structures and procedures are changing in significant ways. As the tort lawyer now knows only too well, it is the administrative lawyer who will inherit the earth. But in doing so, he will be forging a new type of administrative law in a sense quite different from that in which common lawyers have hitherto used the term. Property as a legal concept is perhaps the very last thing likely to help him in his work. The spirit, and some of the procedures, of private law as an adjudicative system are another matter; they should continue to form a defeasible set of presuppositions for what, one hopes, will have the right to be called a system of administrative *justice* and will display some continuity with the Anglo-American tradition of seeing men and women trained in the common law as especially fitted to hear claims, evaluate evidence, and be guardians of civic rights, of impartiality, independence and truth. Otherwise we will indeed plunge headlong into a new feudalism or worse.

2

Frames of reference for legal ideals

W. L. Morison

I A historical sketch

1 Law as the embodiment of common sense
In welcoming an article published in the *Sydney Law Review* in the 1950s, Dean Erwin Griswold of Harvard Law School (writing to the then editor) described it as an 'old line' article and wished that more such papers were published nowadays. What were the characteristics of these 'old line' museum pieces? One commonly heard suggestion is that they were absorbed in technicality, with a lack of appreciation of real issues, and that for this reason there is little occasion to be nostalgic about their passing. This is certainly an oversimplification. There is a good deal less technicality, in the sense of an attempt at a comprehensive summation of the authorities, in the works of older writers like Holmes, Pollock, Dicey or even Anson, than would be found now in many law review articles. What was characteristic of the earlier writings, rather, was a belief in the validity of continuing values, enshrined in the law as they had emerged even in the remote past, accompanied by varying degrees of anxiety about threats to those values from social factors developing outside the law. In Dicey this exhibited itself particularly in his deep suspicions of what he called collectivism, in Pollock in the attempts to pin down such of the law as could be pinned down through codifying various branches of it. He worked assiduously, despite his expressed belief that a statute was by its nature a less effective way of disposing of a problem than a well considered judgment in the same sense.[1]

---

[1] See, for example, A. V. Dicey, *Lectures Introductory to the Study of the Law of the Constitution* (9th edition, London, 1939) introduction by E. C. S. Wade, pp. lxxxviii–xc; A. V. Dicey, *Lectures on the Relation between Law and Public Opinion in England during the Nineteenth Century* (2nd edition, London, 1914, reprinted 1930) introduction and pp. 211–302; Sir Frederick Pollock, 'Judicial Caution and Valour' (1929) 45 *Law Quarterly Review*, pp. 293, 297.

There is no sharp distinction between 'old line' and 'new line' writing in the centrally important respect of the interest shown in the relations between law and society. Men regarded as innovators in Harvard, like Ames, were legal historians. So were Pollock[2] (among other things) and Dicey, even if the latter was concerned more with the recent than the remote past (for example, *Law and Opinion*). Nor were those men, whose writings are the older classics, from our viewpoint now mere historians of doctrine. Pollock annotated Maine's pioneering attempt to correlate the development of various more general features of the law with social conditions in a variety of civilizations;[3] Pollock's Oxford took the legal historians Vinogradoff and Holdsworth to its bosom. Dicey attempted not only to relate legal developments to social conditions in England but to explore Continental comparisons.

Pollock's adverse reaction to the young Roscoe Pound of Harvard— his description of him to Holmes as 'ingenious' was not, in the context, intended to be complimentary[4]—is therefore puzzling at first sight. For there was much that Pound shared with all those already mentioned. His interest in the stages of legal development, and in the situation on the Continent as well as in England and America, was on a scale rather more comprehensive than their own. This was no doubt part of the trouble. The Oxford tradition emphasized care and thoroughness in legal and social research on particular areas or aspects. It was inimical to generalizations on the grand scale. The nature of the generalizations about the springs of legal development which were beginning to appear in Pound's work was certainly more important in exciting suspicion than the fact that generalizations of this degree of comprehensiveness were being made at all.

For the English writers dominant before the First World War, legal argument on controversial matters could be carried on in terms of a background criterion no more ambitious than that of looking to what common sense required in the circumstances (for example, Pollock, 'Judicial Caution', especially p. 295). When Pollock and Anson disagreed about the decision in *Derry* v. *Peek* ((1889) 14 App. Cas. 337), it was to this criterion that they both appealed. Anson said that, if his decision had gone the way Pollock thought it ought to have gone, English law would not be 'a monument of practical common sense'.[5] Pollock did not deny that in general the common law was such a

---

[2] See, for example, F. Pollock and F. W. Maitland, *History of English Law before the Time of Edward I* (1st edition, Cambridge, 1895).

[3] Sir Henry Maine, *Ancient Law* (1st edition, with notes by Sir Frederick Pollock, London, 1906).

[4] 2 *Pollock-Holmes Letters*, edited by M. Dew. Howe (1st edition, Cambridge, 1942), p. 141. *Cf.* the description of Pound as 'monstrous learned but', 1 *Pollock-Holmes Letters*, p. 228.

[5] Sir W. R. Anson, 'Derry and Peek in the House of Lords', (1890) 6 *Law Quarterly Review*, pp. 72, 74.

monument, but on the particular matter he supported, against Anson, what he asserted to be the common opinion of Lincoln's Inn (1 *Pollock-Holmes*, p. 215)—and judicial posterity has agreed with him. Vinogradoff, consistently with this approach, entitled his introductory work for law students *Common Sense in Law* (1913).

This elevation of common sense had two striking and related features. In the first place, common sense was conceived as something very much embodied in the law itself, not as something presenting a set of demands on law that were in any way markedly divergent from the state of the actual law as it was conceived to be. Anson writes of the law as a monument *of* common sense and Vinogradoff of common sense *in* law. In the second place, little philosophical analysis was applied to the concept itself. It was used rather than analysed and this tendency persisted in Oxford to a much later stage, to my own experience as a student.

In both these respects, English legal thinking at the beginning of this century might be considered to have been in a state of decline, perhaps attributable to the aftermath of late Victorian self-satisfaction with the state of the law and with the performance of the elements in English society who were in charge of it. In earlier Victorian times, the question whether the law measured up to standards worked out in terms of philosophical conceptions external to the law itself had been the subject of extended examination by a string of legal philosophers working to elaborate and apply the Benthamite Utilitarian conception of the greatest happiness of the greatest number.[6] But while the Benthamite method of defining the law as it is, by reference to the command of the sovereign, continued to be dominant in English legal writing, interest in Utilitarianism as a method of determining what the law ought to be, as a constant stimulus to law reform, had declined and Dicey was exceptional in this respect (*Law and Opinion*). As Dicey showed (*ibid.* lecture 6), this decline was largely because the particular applications made of Utilitarianism by Bentham and his disciples, while in the first instance salutary in removing obsolete legal restraints on social and economic developments, had been discredited when they were used to support inhumanitarian excesses of the middle classes, whom they had helped to liberate, against the lower classes who became increasingly enslaved to their operations. Consequently, when in the late 1950s Oxford's H. L. A. Hart sought to rebut the charge by Harvard's Lon L. Fuller, that the English positivist tradition was associated with a lack of interest in questions about what the law ought to be, he found himself going back a long way in order to assemble the rebutting evidence.[7]

---

[6] Especially by John Austin, See *Lectures on Jurisprudence*, edited by R. Campbell (5th edition, London, 1885), lectures 3 and 4.

[7] H. L. A. Hart, 'Positivism and the Separation of Law and Morals', (1958) 71 *Harvard Law Review*, p. 593.

2 *Law as adjustment to socio-legal evolution*

Pound's work represented a break away in the direction of emphasis upon ethical questions. His most general definition of law, however, scarcely brings this out. The notion of law as 'the regime of ordering human activities and adjusting human relations through the systematic application of the force of a politically organized society' retains the conception of law as something supported by political power which was central to the positivist approach of Bentham—law as something imposed;[8] it was an approach which survived in English legal thought up to the time when Pound began to write. But it is one of the more specialized notions of law mentioned by Pound which 'he himself seems to have most occasion to use. In this sense law for Pound is 'the aggregate of laws, the whole body of legal precepts which obtain in a given politically organized society'. 'But', Pound adds, 'in a wider phase of this sense it may mean the body of authoritative grounds of, or guides to, judicial and administrative action, and so of prediction of such action, established or recognized in such a society including precepts, technique, and received ideals' (for example, I *Jurisprudence*, p. 12).

Of the three concepts with which the passage just quoted concludes, that of 'received ideals' is, from the point of view of Pound's relationship with the classical English writers, the most important. For it functions in some respect to replace the notion of common sense, itself left amorphous in most of the classical writers and conceived of as spread amorphously through the precepts and techniques. Instead, we are now invited to isolate the ideals of law for study and to consider their relationship to the precepts and techniques. Moreover, the notion that they are 'received' raises the question of the sources from which they are received. In this connection, as in others, Pound envisages that there is involved a process of response to developing social situations, and hence change in or accretion to the ideals over a period. For example, in describing the degree of reception of English law in the early formative period of American law, Pound says that in some cases 'the courts determined what was applicable and what was not by reference to an idealized picture of pioneer rural America of our formative era and this picture became a received ideal' (3 *Jurisprudence*, p. 431; cf. 2, pp. 117–18). Pound conceives an ideal as received when it has 'acquired a certain fixity in the judicial and professional tradition';[9] but he means only, of course, a 'certain' fixity, a fixity in degree, not necessarily a permanent fixity.

[8] See, for example, R. Pound, I *Jurisprudence* (St Paul, Minn., 1959); Jeremy Bentham, *The Limits of Jurisprudence Defined*, edited by C. W. Everett (New York, 1945), p. 88.

[9] R. Pound, 'The Theory of Judicial Decision' (1923) 36 *Harvard Law Review*, pp. 641, 654.

The examination of the ideals embodied in the law at any particular time in this way raises important questions about the frames within which the more fundamental aspects of lawyer's thinking should be carried on. If a particular writer is in general satisfied with the sets of values represented by the law as it stands, it is natural for him to idealize the concept of 'law' or 'the law' itself as a focus in terms of which he organizes the demands he makes. This is particularly so if he feels that set of values threatened by rising forces in society outside the law. I take this to be the position in which the classical writers found themselves. A reformer, on the other hand, may find some values which he supports embodied in the law but he will want to see these kept under examination and he will therefore want to emphasize the impermanence, from his point of view, of at least some of the values embodied in the law. The frame or focus of his thinking about legal ideals is likely to be some concept of society and the way it develops rather than the law itself. This I take to be Pound's position.

Thus, Pound calls upon jurists, as perhaps their most important task, to induce a consciousness in the judges of the role that ideal pictures of the social and legal order play in the development of the law. He places the task of picturing the social order first and describes it as 'to induce a consciousness of the role of ideal pictures of the social and legal order both in decision and in declaring the law' ('Judicial Decision', p. 958).

Pound's notion of the way society and law develop in relation to one another was well adapted to a very moderate reformism. In so far as there is a single notion in Pound's work whose function corresponds to the function served by common sense in the work of the classical English writers, it is the notion of civilization. The task of the legislator or judge is to further and transmit civilization, while that of the jurist is to develop approaches that aid the judge in the 'maintaining, furthering and transmitting of civilization' (1 *Jurisprudence*, p. 287). Pound thought of the development of society as the development of civilization; he saw law ideally as going through phases corresponding to the phases of civilization, as one means of social control rendering the successive stages of civilization effective and secure. He considered that, on the whole, law had performed this function properly and effectively, so that the successive stages of the development of law did in fact reflect the successive stages of the development of civilization. Further, he conceived the development of civilization in a society as proceeding in a more or less continuous evolutionary fashion if one looked at a sufficiently broad time span, and not as a movement taking place in fits and starts, with periods of reaction and of revolution. The same, he thought, was true of law.

On this sort of approach the ideals embodied in the law at any particular time—the 'received' ideals—will be expected to contain much that is of value, at least for the next stage of the process by which law adapts to the development of society. They may even contain large elements of permanent value if it is supposed that evolution takes place by building upon some achievements of the past which retain a degree of identity and are never wholly transformed. Pound indeed made this supposition. He thought of law in a developed society as having proceeded through a number of successive stages, defined as those of primitive law, strict law, equity and natural law, maturity of law and a current fifth stage less easily defined (*ibid.* p. 366). The permanent contribution of primitive law was the idea of a peaceable ordering of the community, that of strict law the idea of certainty and uniformity in the ordering (*ibid.* pp. 405–6, 421), that of the period of equity and natural law the idea of good faith and moral conduct attained by reason (pp. 406, 421), and that of the state of maturity of law probably the idea of individual legal rights (p. 427). The fifth stage added, though not yet as something permanently established, the idea of the importance of securing social interests in the sense of satisfying as much as possible of the sum total of human demand (p. 432). The development of law in these respects is seen as paralleling the development of community ideals as articulated by the community's social philosophers. Thus Pound relies on the philosopher William James for the idea that philosophical thinking in this area has proceeded through stages in which it was first supposed that the end of law was keeping the peace. Then it was asked, why keep the peace? and the answer seemed to be, for the purpose of maintaining the social order. But then the question was raised, why maintain the social order? and the answer was that this makes division of labour possible and sets us free for individual self-assertion. And what, it was then said, is the reason for supporting freedom? and the answer was, because it is a strong human demand and the desirable object for social controls of any kind, law or others, is the maximum satisfaction of human wants (*ibid.* pp. 543–4).

The particular form of evolutionary ethical theory which Pound espoused was well designed not only for a moderate reformism generally, but to enable him to have something of both worlds on the special issue of the most satisfactory frame for consideration of the ideals for law. He saw 'law' or 'the law' as a gathering up of the achievements of the past in the ideals which it represented in his time, and 'law', thought of more generally, as representing in addition successful techniques for adaptation of the law to the requirements of further stages of societal development. Both because of their achievement in securing for society ideals developed in the past and because of their devising means of continuing this, Pound felt a respect for the judges which almost matched in its inducement to feelings of

C

satisfaction Anson's notion of the law as a monument of common sense.[10] At the same time, the veneration which on Pound's theory is due to law, the law and the judge did not depend on any view of law as supporting one set of social ideals against another set. Indeed, his general statement of the objectives of the law of his time would be inconsistent with any such notion, since all demands made on the law from society are treated in a sense as of equal validity for the tasks which lawyers are called on to perform. The springs of the ideals which law is called on to secure are conceived as those of society generally, and the ideals of 'the law' and 'law' are in the first case a record of its success and in the second case a guarantee of the continuance of its success in the service of the ideals of society. 'Law' and 'society' are both concepts thought to embody ideals with which the lawyer must be concerned and any conflict which has to be resolved is thought of as a disequilibrium which may be expected to be only temporary.

3 Law as the struggle of 'right' to consciousness

In the course of time Pound was to be found looking askance at newer legal writers much as the classical English writers had looked askance at him. In article and counter-article[11] he found himself in conflict with the realists, who had proliferated in the period of the First World War, the aftermath of war and the onset of economic depression. All these conditions were conducive to producing dissatisfactions leading to a radicalism beyond Pound's. Yet Pound's work had done much to provide realists with jumping-off points and in those aspects of legal thinking on which I am concentrating here, many of the realists present similarities to Pound. Like him, though in ways in which they differ from one another, most of them managed to reconcile a veneration for law[12] and the legal profession with an insistence on the general societal springs of legal development. Further, in the ways in which they reinterpreted the relationship between law and society, they could be considered as reinterpreting Pound in the direction of what they made of developments outside the law, particularly in psychological theory. Pound's conception of law as a handmaiden to the general forces of social development, no matter how vital its contribution in this respect, readily lent itself to reinterpretation in the light of the notions of psychological behaviourism, in the direction that law was to be thought of as a process of official response to environmental conditions. In Pound, the *process* of legal decision

[10] 'On the whole, our courts have the best record of any of our institutions.' 2 *Jurisprudence*, p. 463. *Cf.* 'Judicial Decision', p. 958.

[11] See R. Pound, 'The Call for a Realist Jurisprudence' (1931) 44 *Harvard Law Review*, p. 697 and K. Llewellyn, 'Some Realism about Realism—Responding to Dean Pound', *ibid.* p. 1222.

[12] See, for example, Llewellyn's hymn to 'The Common Law Tradition' printed in *The Common Law Tradition* (Boston, 1960), p. 399.

appeared as a third meaning of law. The first it will be recalled, the most general, was that of law as a regime of social control; the second (the first more specialized meaning) was that of law as comprising the ideals, precepts and techniques of the law. The third meaning was clearly the least important in Pound's scheme, both in the amount of space which Pound gives to it in his major work on *Jurisprudence* and in the function which it served.[13] For Pound it was the application of the ideals, precepts and techniques.[14] It was otherwise, however, with the realists and here the sharp differences emerge.

In this respect, the extent of difference with Pound varies with the particular realist we are considering. Jerome Frank represents an extreme of difference, since a particular judicial response is considered to be unique to the stimulus provided by the set of environmental conditions to which the judge is responding.[15] Thus not only do the ideals, precepts and techniques of the law fail to explain the pattern in judicial responses but, if the idea is carried to its logical conclusion, there is no such pattern anyhow. The contrast is emphasized by Frank's disrespect for the judges; in his view the judges' failure to recognize that they necessarily bear the responsibility for their own decisions, and their attempts to refer them instead to authorities binding upon them, is a kind of infantilism which Sigmund Freud's theories provide us with the materials for explaining (*Law and the Modern Mind*). Oliphant may be taken as an example of a more 'middle of the road' realist approach. Oliphant, like Frank, decries the influence of law in Pound's second sense on the course of decision, but nevertheless is prepared to find a pattern in the course of decision as it emerges. He demonstrated a greater respect for the judicial fraternity than Frank did, and believed that the judges' experience led them to react in orderly fashion to the different social situations with which they found themselves faced. Hence we can expect to explain the pattern of such decisions by ourselves concentrating on the study of the social sciences, and looking for the principles of judicial action there.[16] The later history of realism since its heyday about the time of the depression seems to consist in a swing to the left by some jurimetricians and a swing to the right by Llewellyn, perhaps realism's most influential exponent.

In some current jurimetrical writing the judge's responses are measured in terms of the predisposing factors arising out of the judge's

[13] Pound's fourth volume of *Jurisprudence* has 503 pages devoted to the analysis of general juristic conceptions and 32 pages to the 'Judicial Process in Action' (chapter 20).

[14] See the alternative title to Chapter 20 in *Jurisprudence* 5.

[15] Jerome Frank, *Law and the Modern Mind* (New York, 1930). See Llewellyn's comment on this aspect of Frank's work in 'Some Realism', pp. 1222, 1231.

[16] Herman Oliphant, 'A Return to Stare Decisis' (1928) 14 *American Bar Association Journal*, pp. 71, 159.

own personal history in relation to the categories of social situation with which the judge is faced in litigation over a period. When the results for the different judges of a court or judicial system are correlated, what is seen to emerge is not any set of general principles of judicial action but rather a profile of the particular court's judicial system.[17] The method of procedure, moreover, discounts the possibility of arriving at a correlation between decisions and the principles purportedly applied in the reasons accompanying a decision. The judge continues to be treated, in the phrase used in criticism of early realism, like Pavlov's dog.

Matters took a different course in the Chicago of Karl Llewellyn, who, in the respects most important for the present topic, is more like Pound than any other realist. Whether this was true of Llewellyn throughout his writing life is a controversial matter which I do not presume to be able to settle. In *The Bramble Bush* he had suggested the overriding importance, for investigation, of what judges do as contrasted with what they say in support of what they do;[18] elsewhere he attacked the biblical statement that 'In the beginning was the Word' by claiming that in the beginning was not a word but a doing ('Some Realism', p. 1222). Yet Llewellyn claimed that these statements in context were reconcilable with attaching particular importance to the judicial pinning-down of ideals in precepts and particularly in the technique by which they do it. Technique was a major object of his inquiry in his later work. He contrasted in this respect the 'grand style', which he approved, and the 'formal style', which he deprecated. The former for him involved a very free use of precedent, the latter a much narrower adherence to the reasons given in the precedents. The former was seen as characteristic of the golden age of Lord Mansfield and others (*Common Law Tradition*, p. 36 and table, p. v; cf. pp. 5–6), the latter as characteristic, with conspicuous exceptions among individuals, of the intervening period up to the relatively recent past (pp. 38–40). But recently the judges, in Llewellyn's view, have been recapturing the grand style if at first largely on the unconscious level. What he saw, therefore, as one of his own immediate missions was to restore judicial confidence by convincing them that they were doing better than they or others knew[19]—that the facts were 'joyous' (*Common Law Tradition*, p. 4)—and to foster the adoption of the grand style among the judiciary at the conscious level.

The insistence on the actuality of a free use of precedent by the judiciary, as well as the insistence on the importance of the distinction between the conscious and the unconscious, preserves in Llewellyn's

---

[17] For example, G. Schubert, *Quantitative Analysis of Judicial Behavior* (New York, 1959).

[18] *The Bramble Bush* (2nd edition, New York, 1951), p. 12.

[19] See, for example, the quotation from T. R. Powell in *The Bramble Bush*, p. 49.

work important lessons of realist thinking. But what rendered him able to escape from the confines of the narrow focus of attention on judicial operations as distinct from judicial thought, which extreme realist thinking might have suggested, was particularly the manner in which he married the modern psychological notion of the unconscious with his own variety of traditional ethical intuitionism. This comes out especially in a consideration of Llewellyn's reasons for supporting the use of the technique of the grand style. For him its usefulness consisted in the manner in which it enabled the judges to work their way towards principles which could not in the first instance be grasped and articulated in a general formulation,[20] although the result which they were ultimately found to dictate might be felt to be the right result in a prior series of individual decisions. But to a larger degree he believed that once success was achieved in articulating at the conscious level a principle which had been exerting its effect in decisions at the unconscious level, it could be seen to be right by a sort of flash of inspiration.[21]

In this way, from a realist point of view interest was re-established, not only in techniques of argument leading to decision and in the struggle for the realization of ideals to be articulated in precepts by such techniques, but also in the ideal content of some precepts embodied in the law as the end product of a successful struggle. Llewellyn continued to think of some factors in individual judicial decisions as unrelated to principles which might turn out to be of lasting value—they were 'equities of the fireside'.[22] But the notion that other factors were responses in terms of intuiting principles—at first on the unconscious level but then consciously at the end of a struggle— was the vehicle of a return to moderate reformism. On this basis the current achievements of the legal profession were treated with some enthusiasm, both on the level of technique and on the level of achieved ideals. Llewellyn wrote a hymn to the common law (*Common Law Tradition*, p. 399) and even a poem about judicial *obiter dicta*, which might in his view come closer to the principle which would ultimately be seen to be right than to the principle on which a case purported to be decided—'Words may be fragrant as they pass.'[23] In one respect, Llewellyn's moderate reformism was more 'practical' than Pound's had been. Llewellyn is said to have been fond of saying, indeed, that

---

[20] 'Response by the court to need—but not yet with understanding', *Cases and Materials on the Law of Sales* (Chicago, 1930), p. 342.
[21] 'The *certainty* in question is that certainty *after the event* which makes ordinary men and lawyers recognize *as soon as they see the result* that however hard it has been to reach, it is the right result', *ibid.* n. 45, pp. 185–6.
[22] *Ibid.* p. 270. *Cf.* p. 157, also called 'the accidental issues and needs of the individual case' in K. N. Llewellyn and E. A. Hoebel, *The Cheyenne Way* (Norman, Okla., 1941), p. 314.
[23] K. N. Llewellyn, *Jurisprudence* (Chicago, 1962), p. 166.

his jurisprudence was the most practical subject in the law course.[24] In the most interesting and urgent areas of legal studies involving the adjustment of law to current social conditions, operation of Pound's scheme of analysis in any thoroughgoing way called for the use of a complex intellectual apparatus. Any attempt to decide a case on the basis of which alternative decision would best further the sum total of human demand to the greatest extent possible is obviously a large undertaking. And while Pound was prepared to offer a group of conceptions which would enable us to work out a scheme of interests to be subserved and to eliminate the necessity of approaching this problem *ad hoc* in the individual case, he was not prepared to apply that method himself in order to present us with the scheme of interests appropriate to the fifth stage of law through which he conceived us to be now passing. He thought this to be premature at the time he wrote (3 *Jurisprudence*, pp. 14–15). We are called on, therefore, to make a variety of comprehensive sociological and philosophical inquiries for ouselves in order to follow Pound's prescriptions and to many this task, though challenging, may appear intractable for everyday purposes. Llewellyn's approach is calculated to emphasize more the value to be gained by examining, though by no means exclusively, the traditional and available legal authorities and struggling to bring to our own consciouness the principles which, with the experience they provide for us and the suggestions they offer, our own intuition will tell us are right. In this way we may hope to train ourselves in arriving at the predictions of future decisions appropriate to the lawyer's task— which Llewellyn contrasts with those of the more general social sciences addressed to the comfortable sweep of the decades—at directing ourselves to what will happen in a case next Thursday (*Common Law Tradition*, pp. 6, 16). In this emphasis on study of the traditional materials, Llewellyn was of course in contrast not only with Pound, but with earlier realists as well. It is said that in the first flush of realism at Yale, its exponents were rarely found in the law school at all: they were out in the New Haven highways examining the psychological responses of motorists to the legal phenomenon of traffic lights.

4 Law as the articulation of reason

What Llewellyn did in Chicago with the weapon of traditional ethical intuitionism, Lon L. Fuller did in Harvard with the weapon of traditional ethical rationalism. For Fuller, as for the realists, law is a process.[25] But this starting point does not involve for Fuller a long

[24] *Cf.* 'I must come up with tools of analysis which any thinking man of law can understand both in their nature and their use, and I must come out with results in words which he can not only understand but put to work', *Common Law Tradition*, p. 516.
[25] Fuller's creature Foster uses this term in *Problems of Jurisprudence* (Brooklyn, N.Y., 1949), p. 82.

process of subsequent reasoning to establish the importance in law of
legal ideals. The notion of ideals as integral to law is inherent in his
notion of the process itself from the beginning. In their differing
notions of what is involved in a 'process', twentieth-century American
legal thinkers reflect the division in Western intellectual tradition
apparent as long ago as in the time of the early Greek Philosophers.
The earlier realists are in the tradition stemming from Heraclitus—
though this emerges more clearly perhaps in the later writings of
Lasswell and McDougal of Yale, when an analysis of the notion of
process came to be used as one method of analysing legal situations.[26]
According to the Heraclitean tradition, reality is flux, and if we see in
its comparatively durable features something more than patterns in
the flux, we are misled. Fuller, on the other hand, belongs to the
tradition of Socrates, Plato and Aristotle. According to this tradition, a
process is a striving towards perfection and this alone makes the
process intelligible.[27] In the case of inanimate objects this notion is to
many people unconvincing: it seems queer to say that there are no
perfect triangles, for example, but the imperfect ones we see would be
perfect, if they could. But in the field of human affairs, as Burnet
remarks, it has very much greater plausibility.[28] It is with human
affairs that Fuller is concerned and he has devoted himself to
demonstrating that his approach is revealing and inspirational not only
in relation to law, but in other human intellectual 'enterprises'[29]—the
term he prefers to 'process'—as well.

More specifically, Fuller sees law as a cooperative human enterprise
directed at a reasoned harmony of human relations.[30] Because of its
appeal to the idea of cooperation and because of its appeal to human
reason, Fuller's thinking shares with Llewellyn's those elements
which we have called, in Llewellyn's case, practical features. In the
lawyer's task of predicting judicial decision, he will be guided on
Fuller's view by the assumption, unless he has special grounds to the
contrary in a particular case, that the judge will be guided by what
justice demands (*Problems of Jurisprudence*, p. 85). And since the
student or lawyer shares a common humanity, and hence a common
human reason, with the judge, he has prospects of working out in
advance what justice does demand. In doing so, he will certainly look
for guidance to the traditional legal authorities as Llewellyn's

---

[26] See, for example, Harold D. Lasswell and Myres S. McDougal, 'Jurisprudence in
Policy-Oriented Perspective' (1966–7) 19 *University of Florida Law Review*, pp. 486,
505.

[27] See especially 'American Legal Philosophy at Mid-Century' (1954) 6 *Journal of
Legal Education*, pp. 457, 470.

[28] John Burnet, *Greek Philosophy Part I—Thales to Plato* (1924 edition, London),
p. 156.

[29] See, for example, *The Morality of Law* (New Haven, Conn., 1964), p. 106.

[30] *The Law in Quest of Itself* (Chicago, 1940), pp. 2–3.

approach requires for, as Fuller puts it, the development of human reason demands attention to what man has made of himself at the present stage,[31] and therefore to what the human legal enterprise has made of itself. But a relatively free use of the authorities is demanded on Fuller's approach as on Llewellyn's, for the flux of judicial decision is only seen as intelligible at all in terms of the objects of striving ('Reason and Fiat', pp. 386–7, 392), which the student must discern in the light of the struggle towards reason which characterizes the enterprise.

Fuller's work represents a highwater mark in a long period of moderate reformism, in its presentation of a concept of 'law' which contains within itself, inherently and by its nature, social ideals to which people wish to commit themselves—ideals, moreover, conceived as being as broad as those of our common humanity. The evolutionary aspect of Pound's thought is preserved in the notion of law as one process of the human realization of man's true or higher nature, without the invitation implicit in Pound's thought to think of the evolution of law as a resonse to social demands external to the law itself, an invitation accepted by the more extreme realists in conceiving of the environment to which legal activity responds as causally more important in legal outcomes than the criteria in terms of which lawyers were traditionally supposed to respond. In Fuller's concept of law, the American ideal of a government of laws and not of men is protected against the notion that the government of law involves its support of the 'establishment' against progress. Fuller's concept gave a theoretical foundation for the statement once heard in Harvard that we cannot understand what the law is unless we know what the law ought to be. Fuller encourages the student, in the student's writing and discussion directed to assist understanding of what the law is, not to exercise care to distinguish his own contribution to its interpretation in the light of what it ought to be from the contributions of those in official positions. The enterprise of law develops in the constant retelling of the story of its development, with no authentic official version (*Law in Quest*, pp. 138–40).

Insofar as we can characterize 'new line' legal writing as distinct from the 'old line' spoken of by Erwin Griswold, it is probably in terms of attitudes to the appropriateness of the approach suggested by the inspirational features common to those writers we have taken as representative of a long and relatively continuous moderate reformism. In terms of such a characterization we will in the course of time come to be as nostalgic about 'new line' writing as Griswold was about 'old line' writing. One detects in general community thinking at the present time, presenting itself as a demand for progress, an association of 'law' with the 'establishment' and an appeal to what is

[31] 'Reason and Fiat in Case Law' (1946) 59 *Harvard Law Review*, pp. 376, 380.

demanded by society or humanity in opposition to what are thought to be the demands of the law. In this kind of thinking law seems to be regarded simply as a set of binding precepts, and as therefore constituting chains which require to be broken if the community is to break free of the trammels of the past. The 'received ideals' in Pound's second meaning of law and the techniques for their adaptation are elements in law to which, as we have seen, other moderate reformists among jurists attached equal importance though in different formulations. On the approach now under consideration they are excluded. Hence law is left, as it were, with little to say for itself, for the features of it which were seen by the writers we have discussed were those which were thought by them to justify it—not because of their theoretically binding quality but in terms of their real value for societal development. Nowadays, community thinking tends to adopt society as a frame of reference for formulating ideals *for* law, which must be implemented by a rapid transformation of it, rather than expecting to find ideals *in* law commanding respect. This is a challenge to our fundamental frames of thinking, calling for critical reappraisal of the type of legal thinking we have been examining as well as some critical appraisal of the type of thinking which is struggling to replace it.

II A critical sketch

In the foregoing I have sought to bring out correlations between the work of particular writers, taken as representative of leaders of legal thought especially in the present century, and particular kinds of traditional ethical theory. Thus English positivism was seen, in its origins at any rate, to be associated with utilitarianism, Pound's sociological jurisprudence with evolutionary ethics, Llewellyn's realism with intuitionism in ethics, and Fuller's natural law approach with rationalism in ethics. This is only a matter of degree in the case of each of the writers concerned. It would not be difficult to detect in each signs of the alternative approaches espoused by others of the writers— for example, to detect in Fuller some reliance on the notion of the unfolding progress characteristic of evolutionary ethics. Nevertheless, if one were to go beyond these writers to other examples of the schools of which they are representative, one would find that the particular kind of ethical association which we have detected in individual writers of a school persists in others of the same school to a degree enabling us to say that it is dominant. Thus, for example, evolutionary ethical theory is dominant in modern sociological jurisprudence, being more strongly apparent in Ehrlich,[32] for example, than it is in Pound. The idea of an intuitive response to a social situation yielding a more

[32] Eugen Ehrlich, *Fundamental Principles of the Sociology of Law*, translated by W. L. Moll (Cambridge, Mass., 1936), discussed in this respect below.

satisfactory result for the judge than a slavish attention to doctrine is by no means confined to Llewellyn among the realists. Bentham's Utilitarianism communicated itself to a number of positivist legal thinkers in England, especially to those who closely followed him like John Austin, but also to later ones. With natural law thinkers like Fuller the connection with rationalism scarcely needs to be argued, since the connection of this kind of thinking about law and ethical rationalism is explicit.

Since these thinkers were, in the central direction of their interests, legal theorists rather than ethical theorists, they tended to devote more attention to carrying out their legal thinking within these ethical frames, than to justifying the ethical frames themselves. They saw urgent problems for the development of law to which they wished in their writings to make an immediate contribution, and one does not concentrate one's attention on the most general problems of navigation when the ship is sinking. Insofar as they sought to justify their general approaches, it was more in terms of their usefulness for achieving objectives in the improvement of the law than in terms of their theoretical validity. But at a time like the present, when more moderate approaches to law reform are the subject of fundamental radical questioning, any vulnerability which these approaches have to theoretical philosophical attack becomes of major importance.

1 *Criticisms of ethical rationalism*

Because the ethical frames in question are of a traditional character, and because ethical matters are traditionally the subject of philosophical division and mutual controversy, each standard type of ethical approach finds itself the subject of standard traditional criticisms. Beginning with the point of view which we have taken Fuller to represent, we may ask, what are the standard criticisms of rationalism? As put by a philosopher influential in the writer's university, they develop along the following lines. We examine the claims of reason to provide us with ideals commanding our allegiance by examining how and why we reason. In the area with which we are here concerned, it is claimed that we reason that we should support a certain course of conduct X (whether by lawgivers or private individuals) because it has the character Y. Then why, the reasoning goes on, do we support Y? We may find ourselves answering, because activities characterized by Y have the character Z. But it is obvious, the argument goes on, that at some point the chain of reasons must stop. And at this point, it is claimed, the reasoner is saying no more than that, if we take Z to be the point where the reasons stop, he supports Y because he is a Z sort of person, because he lives in a certain way, supports this kind of objective.[33]

[33] John Anderson, *Studies in Empirical Philosophy* (Sydney, 1962), p. 352.

It is little different, the argument continues, if we think of the reasoning as proceeding not within a single mind, but between two or more people by way of argument or persuasion. There are conceived to be limits to persuasion and discussion, which can only satisfactorily take place under conditions where there are common ways of living, common demands arising from communicating activities (Anderson, p. 247). The conclusion of the reasoning in this case is the joint assertion of such a common demand and the observation of its relationship to the proposed course of conduct about which the argument began.

In the criticism of rationalism, for which the preceding account of features of the actual reasoning process is designed to provide a basis, it is claimed that rationalism in the first place attempts to obtain a dialectical advantage by ignoring the multiplicity of objectives, ways of living, or movements, which provide the source of norms of conduct for different people and groups. When we tell a person that some action is ultimately demanded by reason, we represent it as favouring what he supports as well as what we support. Even if he remains uncertain about this, we at least confuse his mind by leading it away from the point that reasoning can justify itself only in terms of some source of norms, that source being an objective or a complex of objectives, which will only appeal to him if he happens to share it (cf. *ibid.* p. 250). However, the argument recognizes that, in its refined philosophical form as distinct from its use in popular discussion, rationalism seeks to grapple with the problem of finding a source of norms which must necessarily appeal to all, and the argument then seeks to rebut the rationalist claims in this respect.

Rationalism is seen as claiming that, while men obviously seek conflicting objectives at times, these demands can be distinguished from those constituting man's true, essential, or higher nature. The existence of the contingent or lower demands may even be explained as failure to exercise properly the reasoning powers with which man is equipped to deduce an appropriate course of action from this true nature. Hence arose Bentham's jibe that according to this kind of thinking, the evil man is just a man who asserts falsehoods (referred to *ibid.* p. 228). But in fact the conflicts of objectives between different movements among human beings are real like any other human phenomenon and the distinction rationalists seek to make can only be supported by the assertion of higher and lower levels of reality—on the basis of a distinction between a metaphysical and a physical world. In the Greek writing, in which rationalism as far as our knowledge goes originated, it is so justified. The striving, moving world of Fuller's 'enterprises' is in Socratic theory not being, only becoming: the real world of being is the ideal world towards which the striving takes place, the world of forms with its organizing principle 'the form of the good' (*ibid.* p. 211).

In this criticism of rationalism, the metaphysical solution to the problem of the reconciliation of human conflict with a universal source of norms in universal human nature is asserted to be philosophically unsound. An account could only be given of the relationship between the world of becoming and the world of being if they could be regarded as existing together in a medium which embraces both of them, but to posit such a medium would be to break down the distinction between the two worlds and to envisage their existence in the same way, in the way that is involved in existence in that single medium. The Socratic position is therefore inherently contradictory and unintelligible. The forms themselves are likewise unintelligible, pure universals the function of which is to enable us to assert general features of things in the physical world but about which themselves nothing can be consistently asserted since this would contradict their nature by treating them as things to be characterized, as particular. No explanation can be given of them. Thus Socrates never explains the form of the good except by vague metaphor, and falls back upon the opinion of right-thinking men in the attempt to give it content (*ibid.*).

Colour is lent to this kind of criticism by features of Fuller's work in particular. Fuller describes the ideal towards which the law is considered to be striving in a variety of ways. It is seen in a modest, but not complete, formulation as 'the basic requirements of social living' and more ambitiously as 'the fullest realization of human powers' (*Morality of Law*, p. 5). It is seen again as 'a rational human existence' (*ibid.*) or 'reasoned harmony' (*Law in Quest* p. 3) based on 'human nature itself' (*Morality of Law*, p. 102). The demands of human nature are articulated at the basic level in the principle of 'the common need' (*Problems of Jurisprudence*, pp. 694 ff.) which means 'the common need men would perceive and feel if they knew the facts' (*ibid*, p. 699). But to tell us that an ideal is the 'basic requirements of social living' tells us nothing of what the basic requirements of social living are in the sense of describing them in terms of any content of empirical fact. Nor are we enlightened by the use of the phrase 'the fullest realization of human powers' as to what a physical world in which this realization occurred would be like, nor what a 'rational human existence' would be like, or a reasoned harmony based on human nature itself, nor even how we are to recognize when we have achieved the common need. And what men would perceive and feel as the common need if they knew the facts is certainly something we could never find out on any experimental basis. We therefore do not know whether, if the experiments could be carried out, a common need would be perceived at all. Fuller in fact does not seek to give any of these ideas this kind of concrete content in any general way, and that this cannot be done is put down to the deficiencies of the current state of our understanding. Fuller does provide, in the elaborate hypothetical example of the ruler named Rex, an account of what a failure to measure up to a minimum morality of law would be like (*Morality of Law*, pp. 33–8). But all that appears to emerge is the proposition that minimally laws must be universal, consistent and intelligible in statement and application, which leaves untouched the problem of delineating the substantive content of ideal law.

To these criticisms it might be expected that Fuller would make the answer that the writer has been presenting criticisms of a view which is in fact not his. He writes in one place that 'we know in advance that we cannot reach our goal of a social order founded solely on reason. But we know equally well that it is impossible to set in advance a stopping place short of our goal beyond which all effort will be in vain. The illusion of natural law has at least this presumption in its favour, that it liberates the energies of men's minds and allows them to accomplish as much as they can' (*Law in Quest*, p. 110). We may answer, however, that it is one thing to set our sights on a definite goal which is too high for complete achievement in the hope of reaching some degree of approximation to it, it is quite another to postulate a goal which must remain forever undefined because the notion of human reason being able to work it out is theoretically unsound. If Fuller thinks of natural law as an illusion in this sense, but useful in liberating energies, the restrictions which this view would impose on clear scholarly communication would have to be offset against whatever advantages might accrue in other directions. In another respect too, Fuller might be expected to claim that our criticisms are misdirected, for he treats it as 'a mistake of the older natural law school', and of some modern scholars, to reach 'abstract resolutions on ends and then to trace out the implications of those resolutions for the various branches of the law' ('American Legal Philosophy', pp. 457, 479). Fuller himself regards the ideal world of values and the world of fact as inextricably intertwined in a single moving reality. To this we may reply that it is no answer to the problem of how facts and values conceived in this way could be related to one another in a single world merely to insist that they do exist together. The problem of rendering intelligible the notion that the moving reality involves such a relationship remains unsolved.

2 Criticisms of ethical intuitionism

At all events, to some moral philosophers of the past it has seemed that the intuitionism on which Llewellyn relies—the idea of a principle which may be difficult to sweat into conscious clarity, but which is immediately seen to be right when expressed[34]—is indefensible in the

---

[34] See, for example, *Cheyenne Way*, p. 330 and his reference to rules which 'make sense on their face', *Common Law Tradition*, p. 38.

same way as rationalism, but more obviously so. Bentham says: 'The various systems that have been formed concerning the standard of right and wrong, may all be reduced to the principle of sympathy and antipathy. One account may serve for all of them. They consist all of them in so many contrivances for avoiding the obligation of appealing to any external standard, and for prevailing upon the reader to accept the author's sentiment or opinion as a reason for itself.'[35] While this criticism may apply equally to rationalism and intuitionism, at least in the case of rationalism the author's sentiment seeks to justify itself by reference to general human nature; it is only at the end of a long dispute with the rationalist that one might come to the conclusion that reason in matters of moral argument can only function in relation to some demand or 'sentiment' personal to the author of the argument or shared between himself and those with whom he is arguing. But in the case of the intuitionist the idea that some kinds of convictions of rightness are a guarantee of their own correctness tends to be put forward as dogma, and it seems to be so in Llewellyn's case. And any attempt to break down the distinction between conviction and truth or correctness can only be obscuring philosophically.

The moral philosopher Sidgwick does indeed distinguish between dogmatic and philosophical intuitionism but, insofar as philosophical justifications of intuitionism have been attempted, they have generally involved the same kind of appeal to metaphysics into which rationalism in its classical versions has been driven, with the same kind of resulting philosophical problems of establishing relationships between different worlds. Thus the intuitionist Butler[36] set up a special faculty of the mind described as conscience, the decrees of which were supposed to possess a higher authority than the decrees of the ordinary passions. But since conscience was disinterested by its nature and passions were interested by their nature, demonstration of how one could move to influence the other presented a seemingly insoluble problem. Butler purported to solve it by the conception of a self-love which mediated between conscience and the passions, seeking the happiness of the mind through reconciling the demands of the passions for their external objectives with the demands of duty laid down by conscience. But this merely substitutes the problem of how three quite different worlds can be related to one another for the problem of finding how two can be.

It seems questionable whether Llewellyn is in any better position by positing special authority in terms of 'rightness' for those decrees which have been arrived at by a process in which the assertion of a principle at the conscious level is the outcome of a process in which the

[35] *Introduction to the Principles of Morals and Legislation* (1823 edition, London), chapter 2, cited Anderson, p. 228.
[36] Joseph Butler, *Fifteen Sermons* (London, 1726).

principle, as it were, fights its way up from the unconscious. The fact that such a principle ultimately gets the conscious seal of approval may indicate that it reconciles for the time being various demands within the personality of the individual legal reasoner or the group where, as in the case of the development in a line of judicial authority, it is a group effort. But there seems nothing in Freud's theories which would suggest that any more is involved here than perhaps very temporary adjustment of conflict, of a conflict which could break out again when factors of which the person or group was unaware at any level came to exert their influence and when what was previously the 'right' principle might no longer seem 'right' to the very same people in terms of their very same demands.

3 Criticisms of ethical Utilitarianism

If, however, we find substance in Bentham's criticisms of intuitionism, it does not necessarily follow that his own Utilitarianism, influential in positivist legal thought as we have indicated, is in any better position, despite its claims to find an external standard guaranteeing the rightness of a course of action, legal or otherwise. 'What one expects to find in a principle', Bentham said, 'is something that points out some external consideration as a means of warranting and guiding the internal sentiments of approbation and disapprobation' (*Introduction to the Principles of Morals and Legislation*, chapter II, cited Anderson, p. 228). But it has seemed to some that the only way of 'warranting' or 'guiding' our internal sentiments is by appealing to others of our internal sentiments, even if in terms of pointing out some external situation which has an appeal to those other internal sentiments (Anderson, pp. 228–30). Nor does it seem that Utilitarianism, thought of as reducible to a kind of intuitionism if the validity of this criticism of it is accepted, is any more defensible in that form than other kinds of intuitionism. The Utilitarian criterion for the rightness of actions is the contribution of a projected course of conduct, including a projected legislative act, to 'the greatest happiness of the greatest number'. But the objectives of a sentiment so described turn out not even to be intelligible. 'Happiness' or 'pleasure', as Bentham's catalogue of pleasures shows (*Introduction*, p. 33), turns out to be no more than what we like or want and the mere enumeration of wanted things gives us no means of estimating the relative worth of different possible courses of action over others, of working out the total of pleasure involved in one possible course of action as compared with the total involved in another (Anderson, p. 231). Economists have found it possible indeed to plot the *relative* keenness of demands in particular individuals by reference to what they do in different situations, and likewise to estimate the relative keenness of demands among particular individuals where it is possible to observe their interactions in some market. But this progress in investigation was achieved only by abandoning the Benthamite notion of quantities of pleasure in the abstract with which economists began, and there is no total human market which could serve to reinstate in intelligible terms the idea of making any general estimate of the quantities of pleasure attached to particular kinds of human activity.

4 Criticisms of evolutionary ethics

This line of criticism is important not only in relation to the ethical frame of some of the thinking of legal positivism, but also because it sets problems for Pound's hypothesis about the fundamental objectives of the fifth and current stage in socio-legal evolution. Pound states this to be 'seeking to satisfy the maximum of the whole scheme of human desires or expectations (or wants, or demands) so far as it may be done through the legal order without too much sacrifice' (1 *Jurisprudence*, p. 543). In another of his formulations the present object of social control is to 'reconcile these desires, or wants, so far as we can, so as to secure as much of the totality of them as we can' (*ibid.* p. 544). Again, he puts it that we must satisfy 'as much of' human demand as we can satisfy with a minimum of friction and waste, with 'the least sacrifice of the totality of interests' (3 *Jurisprudence*, p. 334). There seem to be assumptions made in much of this language that a general calculus of human pleasures is an intelligible notion, in which case Pound's approach to current problems may be vulnerable to the criticisms advanced against Bentham's ethics on general theoretical grounds, to which added colour is lent by historical trends in economic theory. If so, Pound is chasing a chimera.

It is no answer to this criticism to say that society is itself a market in which the respective keenness of different human demands, at any rate in that society, is demonstrated by the actual results of their interaction. If in this sense society does serve as a market in the way a market in the more ordinary sense serves the purpose of economic investigation, nevertheless, it is not the sort of market which will serve as a criterion for the rightness either of conduct or measures of social regulation. On such a criterion, the notion of society as it ought to be would be amalgamated with that of society as it is, and this would satisfy few ethical thinkers and certainly not Pound himself. Nor is it what Pound appears to envisage. The criterion is not society as we have it, but rather the society which is coming to be—the society in which changes taking place now will issue in some degree of equilibrium. It may be plausible to suppose that we could, with sufficient information about current causal factors and the field in which they are operating, arrive at a prediction of the features of that equilibrium situation which might serve as an incentive to us to throw our weight into the cause of advancing the future social and legislative progress. For this to be regarded as necessarily indicating to us what is right, however, it would be necessary for us to think that what will emerge in the near future will necessarily be better than what exists now. This is in fact an assumption made by evolutionary ethical theory, which we believe to be represented by Pound's general approach, and therefore calls for examination here.

Any theory of ethics as evolutionary would appear to bear a heavy onus of proof in the light of what we seem actually to observe in the study of history generally, especially if we take broad time spans. What we seem to observe in the history of civilizations is periods of barbarism intervening between periods of culture, stages of growth and stages of decay. Pound, in explaining the stages of development of law, himself finds parallel stages of growths in laws belonging to different periods of human history in general, which we would perhaps think of as periods of civilization as opposed to barbarism. The logical implication is that in the case of the older ones, as distinct from our present one, periods of growth were succeeded by stages of decay or disruption, and indeed the reason why Pound is only able to speculate cautiously about the next stage of our law, is that disruption of the older ones occurred before the stage of maturity of law had been transcended. Any historical process, social or otherwise, has on any scientific approach a beginning and an end. The notion of a permanently improving social process, in which each stage is a necessary introduction to the next stage and has a subordinate goodness on that account, is unhistorical and unscientific. The idea which Pound puts forward as his goal of law for our own era is a logical development from the previous stages. Yet that goal is substantially the Utilitarian Benthamite goal, so highly influential one hundred and fifty years ago, and this calls attention to the dubious account of actual cultural history by which Pound seeks to give the notion of evolution plausibility. Nor is Pound's notion of the goal as achievement of a sum or average of societal demands any invention even of Bentham. The Utilitarian idea appears fully fledged in writers prior to Bentham,[37] and the general notion appears in the position taken by Glaucon in Plato's *Republic* (book II, referred to in Anderson, p. 227).

The unscientific character of evolutionary ethical doctrine is obscured in the minds of some by the supposition that it is connected with the views of that respected nineteenth-century innovator in the field of natural sciences, Charles Darwin. Yet ultimately the evolutionary ethical approach is opposed to Darwin's and in line with the approaches of earlier thinkers, with antiquarian prototypes in the theories of Parmenides, the father of materialism, and Anaxagoras, but

[37] See, for example, 16 *International Encyclopedia of the Social Sciences*, edited by D. L. Sills (New York, 1968), p. 224 and bibliography p. 229.

stemming more immediately in the modern period from Hegel, especially through Marx. In Darwin's approach, the relationship between a thing and its environment is not absolutely fixed, and in any struggle it is logically just as possible that the environment will give way and not the thing environed, or vice versa. On the other hand, what is characteristic of evolutionary ethics in its own historical development is the supposition of a dualism between man and nature, in which overwhelming forces are supposed to be at work on one side or the other—the side which represents the true reality while that of the other is only dependent. The contest between the Hegelians and the Marxists in the general philosophical area is about the question on which side the overwhelming forces lie.

In Hegelianism history is seen as the development of universal spirit towards the rationality which is its essential nature through stages, in each of which contradictions are solved by the dialectical process of thesis, antithesis and synthesis, at successively higher levels of rationality. Spirit, or mind, has a reconciling mission, though the reconciliations which it effects are not seen as reconciliations between conflicts existing in things independent of mind, but as reconciliations of conflicts in the mind itself (cf. Anderson, pp. 79–87). The mind is the fundamental stuff of reality, its movements are the movements of the totality. In classical Marxist thought, in contrast with Hegelian, the fundamental reality is in matter rather than in mind, and it is in the material world that the overwhelming forces of evolution lie. The ideal world is nothing else than the material world reflected by the human mind and translated into forms of thought.[38] Seeing idealism and materialism as the two fundamental tendencies in philosophy, the classical Marxists reject the subjectivism of the former, in which bodies can only be sensations sprung from the mind, and fall back on the objectivity of fundamental matter. But the Hegelian notion of evolution and especially societal evolution through stages, characterized by the dialectical process posited by Hegel, is retained.

Classical Marxism thus shares with Hegelianism the notion of a moving totality, and attaches features to that totality which are more plausibly attached to it when the totality is thought of as fundamentally mental than when it is thought of as fundamentally material in the Marxist fashion. Reality is perceived as developing through a process of logic, proposition (thesis) and counter-proposition (antithesis) followed by solution (synthesis) until the argument breaks out again at the next higher stage. Contradictions thus occur in the material world itself, leaving the inquirers into it without the tests which may ordinarily be employed to establish who is right and who is wrong in arguments in the ordinary sense between people. Ultimately this must lead, as in the older established version of

[38] Karl Marx, preface to the second edition of *Capital*, quoted Anderson, p. 302.

Hegelianism, to scepticism which, however, the Marxist does not embrace (cf. Anderson, pp. 306–11). But even if he does not, the effect is to subvert the scientific faith in a reality in which the regular operation of cause and effect permit the discovery of scientific principles. Moreover, the classical Marxist must attribute a design or purpose to reality which again would be more plausible if we supposed it to be mental after the manner of the older Hegelians. Thus Karl Kautsky claims that 'it was the materialist conception of history which has first completely deposed the moral ideal as the directing factor of social evolution, and has taught us to deduce our social aims solely from the knowledge of the material foundations.'[39] Clearly, social aims can only be 'deduced' from the material foundations if the material foundations have their own aims (Anderson, p. 321). In fact in spite of Marx's materialism man and society are in practice the subject of his history and the rationalizing of things is identified as their 'coming to consciousness'.

But, whatever may be said about the consistency with which Hegel and Marx and their disciples adhere to their opposing views of the fundamental nature of the moving totality, the major point of criticism of evolutionary ethics in general must be made in relation to the assumption which they explicitly share—the assumption of a totality of things moving inevitably in the direction of rationality. In ordinary language, when we distinguish change from what changes, we are clearly not thinking of what changes as something eternal. It is only if we think of the substance of change, what changes, as itself a pattern of processes that we can indeed think of 'it' changing. We can then think of the discontinuance of some processes which do not affect the pattern as we are envisaging it; but we know that what we think of as in this sense the subject of change will also be a stage in the changes of some other pattern. We not only do not have to hypothesize some substance as the subject of *all* changes, but to do so would appear to involve us in insoluble problems to explain how changes could be attributed to *it*. In its attitude to change, evolutionary ethics is in the tradition stemming from Socrates, Plato and Aristotle and opposed to the Heraclitean. And in this respect, it appears to be subject to those philosophical criticisms which we have already put forward in criticism of the older forms of rationalism. It is a doctrine of higher-level reality, posing insoluble problems in regard to the manner in which the higher level of reality is to be conceived as related to what we actually observe taking place.

III Some conclusions for the present time

The foregoing sketches have been presented in the belief that the matters canvassed have relevance to current notions about ideals for

[39] Karl Kautsky, *Ethics and the Materialist Conception of History*, translated by J. B. Askew (Chicago, 1914), p. 201.

law which are influencing present legal development and pose problems for the immediate future. At the conclusion of the first section it was suggested that current community thinking tends to adopt society as a frame of reference for formulating ideals *for* law, which must be implemented by transformation of it, rather than to seek ideals *in* law commanding respect. Law teachers are likely to find that, if a class is considering material of some judge or author who appeals for support to the law considered as an object to which veneration or respect is due by the nature of it, the dominant reaction is scornful laughter. If, however, a judge or author appeals to 'society' in the same manner and with the same object, the reaction of students is one of approval. In the community generally, widespread demands are heard that existing states of affairs or proposed courses of action must be justified by reference to their 'social relevance'.

If 'society' is here to be understood in accordance with the most general presupposition of evolutionary ethical doctrine, then theoretically nothing at all can be justified on grounds of social relevance. The notion of society which is being set up is a metaphysical one and nothing in the ordinary world of experience can be demonstrated to have any logical relationship to it. Moreover, it appears that in much that is said such assumptions are in fact being made. It would be almost as unthinkable that a government in any Western society should declare itself to be against progress as it would be that it should declare itself to be against goodness or justice. If a particular change is attacked, it is likely to be on one of two major grounds. It may be said first that the particular change is reactionary, that it involves a reversion to the past or seeks to consolidate the position of a group 'established' by past history. Alternatively, a measure may be attacked on the ground that it seeks to bring about change in an undesirable or inefficient manner or at the wrong time. Changes may be said to be going on too rapidly, and particular ones may be said to require deferment until 'we can afford it.'

While appeals to the basic presuppositions of evolutionary ethics flourish, the attempts to reconcile these presuppositions with respect for the received ideals of the existing order weaken in popular thought and official action. In popular thought the matter may be illustrated by the sharp contrast between attitudes to conservationism and conservatism. So much emphasis is laid on conservation that it may be called, in John Searle's terms, one of the 'sacred issues' of our time.[40] Conservationism is directed towards the preservation of the beauty of the physical environment, the prevention of exploitation of it by industry to the destruction of resources which work to the economic advantage and amenity of other groups, and the preservation of

[40] John R. Searle, *The Campus War* (New York, 1971).

artificial structures thought to be of permanent value— the 'national estate'. It is clearly not directed to the preservation of intangible values embodied in existing social arrangements such as law—the 'heritage of ideas'—always excepting democracy.

It was likewise different, forty years ago, in respect of popular and intellectual attitudes to matters which influence official action more directly. Among these we may list attitudes involving what Wesley Hohfeld called 'fundamental legal conceptions'.[41] In Hohfeld's theory the laying down of legal rules involves the establishing of rights by one person or institution accorded legal personality, against another person or institution accorded legal personality, or giving the one against the other privileges, powers or immunities, each of which notions has a logical relationship to rights. Hohfeld emphasized that the giving of a right logically involved imposing a duty on the person against whom the right was established. What was established was the setting up of a relationship in which one party's position was described as a right and the other's as a duty. The terms were correlative, in the same way as what Hohfeld called a no-right (what might be a little more elegantly termed an exposure) was correlative with a privilege, a liability with a power, and a disability with an immunity. For Hohfeld it was essential to clarity of thought that we should always recognize that the assertion of one party's position in the relationship involved the assertion of the correlative position of the other party, but mistakes were in fact constantly being made about this to the confusion of the law.

Hohfeld's analysis appears to be equally applicable in circumstances where it is claimed that rights, privileges and the like are established by rules of other kinds, such as political or moral rules, which are said to be recognized or to call for recognition on some basis disclosed or undisclosed. It is applicable, firstly, in the respect that such claims to the existence of rights must logically involve claims to the existence of the correlative duties, and likewise with the other pairs of correlative notions. It is applicable, secondly, in the respect that we must expect to find in these areas a degree of confusion about this, as Hohfeld demonstrated there was in legal areas. At least we seem to find that at particular times attention in the prevailing climate is concentrated upon one person's or body's position in the relationship which the correlatives describe and scant explicit regard is given to the position of the other person or body.

In this last respect, there was forty years ago a marked contrast in Anglo-Saxon countries between where the emphasis was placed in matters regarded as political and those regarded as moral. In political matters the emphasis was heavily on the rights of the citizen against the

---

[41] W. N. Hohfeld, *Fundamental Legal Conceptions* (New Haven, Conn., 1923).

state. Moreover, the rights of the citizen were conceived to have been largely established by existing political arrangements of one kind or another, legal or at least conventional. History was presented largely as political history, dealing with the growth of democracy generally, the political emancipation of minority groups, the ultimate recognition of the political rights of women, and the securing by the state of freedoms in particular areas of activity—freedom of speech and the like. When reference was made to duties, it was likely to be to the duties of preservation of the system especially against external attack.

In those areas regarded as pertaining to morality on the other hand, the emphasis was very heavily on duties. These duties were often expressed in ways which implied that they existed in a context of satisfactory social and political arrangements. A respected essay on ethics bore the title 'My Station and its Duties'.[42] At a time when many more children engaged in religious observances, they sang that Jesus bade them shine 'you in your small corner and I in mine', or more briefly, in another hymn, to 'brighten the corner where you are'. If children did not engage in religious observances, they were likely to be exposed nevertheless to similar demands from such figures as Walt Disney's Pinnochio. People were expected to be preoccupied with their own duties to their neighbours, and not to show concern with the rights against their neighbours which a general system of duties of neighbour to neighbour logically implied.

In the 1960s the leading legal philosophers Hart and Fuller[43] were still emphasizing in their respective works 'a morality of duty'; while this was regarded as only a minimum morality, the contrast made was not with a morality which approached these matters from the point of view of rights, but with a morality of 'aspiration' (Hart, pp. 166–78; *Morality of Law*, chapter 1), an approach accommodated by the popular thinking of the previous age anyhow, through such phrases, common in panegyrics, as 'service beyond the call of duty'. Yet by now to treat duty as the foundation of morality was coming to seem curiously out of touch with the prevailing climate of thought. A process of welding together of political and moral approaches especially under the concept of 'human rights' was gathering increasing strength throughout the Anglo-Saxon countries as elsewhere.

The historical process of democratization was now seen as an unfinished evolution. History was less and less political history, more and more social and economic history. Political history itself was presented with less emphasis on explanations in terms of political personalities and more on underlying social and economic trends. There was less emphasis in general teaching of the young on history at

[42] F. H. Bradley, *Ethical Studies* (2nd edition, Oxford, 1927) essay 5.
[43] H. L. A. Hart, *The Concept of Law* (Oxford, 1961). Fuller, *Morality of Law*.

all and more on broader social studies. The old man finds himself now at cross purposes with the young man in a discussion of the distribution of power in the community. For the old man the term naturally refers to the supposedly equally distributed political power. For the young man it naturally refers to the patently unequally distributed economic power and the political implications thereof. Democracy now comes to be demanded as a collection of rights applying to institutions of society generally, like those which are thought to influence government and those which affect the lives of the individual in different ways, such as educational institutions.

The older bills of rights, whether the British document of the seventeenth century or the amendments to the American constitution of the eighteenth, laid particular emphasis on establishing the rights of the citizen against the state. Present day proposals seek to establish the rights of citizen against citizen equally importantly. Indeed, under the proposals of the Australian Attorney-General of 1973, the Australian parliament was to occupy a unique position in that its future laws were not to be subject to invalidation if inconsistent with the provisions of the proposed act. Perhaps the primary drive of the proposed legislation was to establish the minimum moral rights to which a citizen was conceived to be entitled against his neighbour as legal rights.

If the Hohfeldian analysis is valid, a system of rights which applies generally among neighbours implies a general system of duties among neighbours. Insofar as this is its effect, a bill of rights might equally be called a bill of duties. It never is. For the person to whom the package is offered is expected to concentrate his attention on the former rather than the latter. In the Australian bill mentioned, the infringer of human rights was to be virtually *caput lupinum*, for the carefully defined rights of the person charged with a criminal offence did not apply to him. The weapon of the civil injunction made available against him could lead to his incarceration through contempt proceedings, whose operation was largely to be in the discretion of a special court. Yet in considerable controversy about the bill, this aspect went unnoticed.

By contrast with the picture we have presented of the position half a century ago, the demand for the legislative securing of basic moral rights is almost by implication associated with dissatisfaction with existing legal and social arrangements. Morality is no longer a matter of fitting in the appropriate manner into an appropriate place in a stable system, but rather the implications for one's own betterment in a better system. In this attitude it seems that sometimes the motive of escape from the existing system operates more powerfully than the attractions of a new one in any way specifically envisaged. Hence it seems that quite illusory changes may have an appeal, rather after the fashion of the placebo in medicine. An adviser who had formulated a rule in a new bill of rights, presented to the public for consideration, was asked what difference it would make to the existing law. He needed to reflect, but finally said it would probably make none at all.

One of the attractions of evolutionary ethical theory is that it appeals to the victims of a vague malaise, to those who do not know what they want and will not be happy till they get it. It offers the hope of a brighter future without necessarily specifying the characterization of a brighter future. But its metaphysical absence of content operates to permit association with it of quite specific demands presented as part of the order of the society of the future. A tension is postulated between the future society and the current one. This is conceived as giving rise to rights of citizens and groups which demand recognition by the current society, and its manager the state, in the interests of progress. At this point there is some mingling of thought in the approach from evolutionary ethics and that from social contract theory, a comparatively modern variety of rationalist ethics. For insofar as the duties correlative with these rights are thought about at all they tend to be fixed on society or the state and social contract notions make the effort to give some sense to this idea.

Yet social contract theory appears to be in no better case than other forms of rationalist ethics to achieve this object. It may be seen as an attempt to delineate the relevant aspects of the nature of man with which rationalist ethics is concerned by examining what man would agree to as a condition of joining society assuming he would weigh the benefits of social cooperation against what he would have to surrender. The standard criticism of such an approach is that the supposition contradicts facts about some human nature we actually know. If it were not the case that human cooperation occurs 'naturally', and not as the result of calculation, a man in the 'original position' would have no means of knowing what the benefits of social cooperation might be (see, for example, Anderson, p. 345). It makes no difference to the force of this criticism whether a social contract is supposed to have actually taken place, or whether it is conceived to be merely the starting point of the construction of a theoretical model as in the recently presented theory of John Rawls.[44] The problem remains as to why certain characteristics are chosen to the exclusion of conflicting ones as the basis of justification for the social arrangements advocated.

An aspect of the current crisis of law, morals, and political ideology is therefore the loss of confidence in the 'received' ideals of law, morals and political ideology and their replacement by recourse to dubious ethical argument. Whatever else has progressed, ethical theory has not. The changes are rung on traditional fundamental notions, singly or in combination. Reflection on the uncharted sea into which such

[44] *A Theory of Justice* (Cambridge, Mass., 1972).

conceptions throw us gives a hollow ring to claims in the highest quarters that the experts must be allowed to tell us what our needs are. Clarity of thought demands that we examine where we 'really' get our values from in terms of our own personal, political, moral and social history and experience, as a precondition to examining in what respects existing political, moral and social arrangements are at odds with them.

Some material in this chapter was originally published in 2 *Dalhousie Law Journal* 3 (1975).

3

Socialism, anarchism and law

Eugene Kamenka
and Alice Erh-Soon Tay

I

There is in advanced industrial or 'post-industrial' societies today, we have written elsewhere,[1] a widespread crisis in law and legal ideology which goes to the very core of social conceptions and hence of 'philosophical' discussion of the nature and function of law and its relation to society. The philosophy of law as the logical analysis of legal propositions and arguments may be another matter, but the theory and nature of justice—or of administration—cannot be discussed as an abstract atemporal question, as something to be treated apart from the macro-sociology of law, from actual demands, actual social expectations and actual social and legal institutions and arrangements. The current crisis illustrates this.

Lawyers, of course, have long been aware of important changes in modern social and economic life, and in modern social and political attitudes, that affect the character and principles of many areas of private law and which have been fundamentally altering the balance between private and public law. They speak, as the late Wolfgang Friedmann did, of a shift from private law, concerned with security of the individual, to public law, concerned with welfare and social utility. Even in the heart of the private law, in the law of tort or torts, and in contract, they have discerned similar developments. In torts, there is the movement from the legal-individualistic principle of fault liability to the social, actuarial cost-benefit analysis that leads to the principle of loss distribution; in contract, the concept of a bargain struck

[1] 'Beyond Bourgeois Individualism: The Contemporary Crisis in Law and Legal Ideology', a paper presented to the Madrid World Congress on Philosophy of Law and Social Philosophy, held in September 1973; reprinted in Eugene Kamenka and R. S. Neale (eds), *Feudalism, Capitalism and Beyond* (London and Canberra, 1975), pp. 126–44. The three paragraphs that follow are drawn from that article. The reader interested in a fuller presentation of our conception of the distinction between *Gemeinschaft*, *Gesellschaft* and bureaucratic–administrative ideologies and arrangements and their bearing on the crisis in Western conceptions of law should consult that volume, esp. at pp. 135–41.

between ideally equal and freely contracting parties is increasingly infringed upon by the court's recognition of social and economic inequalities and of the one-sided restriction of the power to bargain by the existence of standard contracts. We have the emergence of whole new areas of law—industrial law, conciliation and arbitration, rent and price control, tenant and consumer protection, safeguarding of the environment—which require conceptions of the nature and function of law and of the nature and procedural characteristics of justice that diverge sharply from the traditional attitudes, concepts and procedures of nineteenth-century common law judges and courts. For a period common lawyers, at least, attempted to save such traditional concepts while accommodating the new developments, by distinguishing law from regulation, courts from tribunals, justice from administration. Today—and this is part of the crisis—the distinction becomes less and less tenable. We are moving in many areas, indeed, to seeking a systematized law of social provinces rather than of individual actions—the law of commerce instead of the law of commercial wrongs, the law of broadcasting, fisheries, mining, and even of the family.

The crisis, of course, has larger social, political and moral dimensions. But these are still not external to law; they lie at the very heart of it. Those lawyers who noted the gradually increasing importance, in the twentieth century, of state regulation, of public law and of considerations drawn from the ideology of welfare and social utility, thought until recently that this was part of an orderly, evolutionary process of socializing and humanizing capitalism, that it could be legitimated and directed in terms of the quasi-individualistic, quasi-social ideology of Benthamite Utilitarianism and piecemeal social engineering. But the development of parallel or competing systems of private and public law, law and administration, courts and tribunals, protection of the legal primacy of the individual and of the primacy of the socio-technical norm carries with it a confrontation of explicit or implicit ideologies, of ways of viewing both law and the world. These are not easily reconcilable into a single system of law or of moral and social philosophy, but do lay claim to each other's areas, do seek to inherit the earth. The resolution of private and public interest attempted by Benthamite Utilitarianism no longer carries conviction to many. (Bentham, after all, like many a welfare administrator, thought that the concept of inalienable rights was nonsense on stilts, and promptly relied on the concept of property to do the work that rights do in other philosophies.) The increasing social visibility of public law and of the need for public law ideology cannot fail to undermine, or at least to revolutionize, the field of private law and its ideology and with it the respect for specifically legal ideals. The last few years, indeed, have made it obvious that the legal developments are signs and parts of a wider crisis—of a renewed crisis in classical liberalism and liberal democracy, in the ideology of free enterprise and of middle-class culture, and in its separation of the moral, the political and the social, made evident in the radical upheavals of the late 1960s. Those upheavals saw a remarkable and largely unexpected revitalization of a highly moralistic revolutionary socialism as a radical critique of society, drawing on a wider concern for the interests, the rights and the dignity of the comparatively poor and underprivileged, both in the national and the international context. Socialists have been able to make some no doubt very familiar, but nonetheless potent, criticisms of law and lawyers as abstract, oriented to the needs and opportunities of the middle class, and so on, but they have done so with only a partial appreciation of the problem and of the trend of events. For the crisis of law and legal ideology is not merely part of the revitalization of socialist hostility to the entrepreneurial society or to its successor, the world of multinational corporations: it is a crisis deeply rooted in nineteenth- and twentieth-century developments—in the course and social ramifications of scientific and technological progress, in the changing conditions of economic production and use, in the vastly increased scale and power of enterprises, in the consequent ever more obvious social interdependence of individuals and units and the growing power of the state and its agencies. The extent to which radical socialists have not fully grasped the point can be seen from the fact that the crisis is not at all confined to the West or to free enterprise societies. It is also to be found in the communist world. There it manifests itself as a crisis within Marxist legal ideology and within the socialist conception of the goal—the spontaneously cooperative, egalitarian, truly human society. The early Marxist-Leninist vision of ultimate communism, in which the government of men is replaced by the administration of things, in which coercive external norms will give way to the settled operation of an internalized consciousness of social and ethical justice, has disintegrated. The crisis in that vision has been dramatized by the bitter struggle between the bureaucratic-administrative realism now espoused by Soviet theorists of law and public administration, and the Maoism of the period of the great proletarian Cultural Revolution, with its emphasis on popular participation, the 'mass line' and great leaps forward, on continuous or recurrent social upheavals under the slogan 'Smash All Permanent Rules, Go One Thousand Li A Day'. The struggle is a struggle between two central but contradictory elements in Marxism—technological rationality versus peasant anarchism, in China itself between the so-called 'capitalist roaders' and the 'gang of four'.

In the communist world, the tension is between revolutionary transformation and the desire for social stability, between mass campaigns and the provision of social and psychological security for individuals, social spheres and activities, between utopian spontaneity and technical-administrative realism. In the West, the crisis is a crisis in the individualistic view of society, in a legal model attuned to the needs of the individual house- or property-holder, the entrepreneur, the settled citizen living on terms of equality with those around him, secure and confident as an individual in his bearing vis-à-vis the state and the rest of society. Against this, the new demands elevate the interests or 'requirements' of the comparatively poor or under-privileged as contrasted with those who are 'at home' with law, they pit the interests of 'society' or of 'humanity' against 'excessive' respect for abstract individual rights and powers, especially proprietarial rights and powers, they tend to see men as social products and not as free moral agents, as people to be cured or helped rather than judged. The new demands are suspicious of lawyers as a profession—in the common law world because they see them as a privileged caste with guild traditions and powers, in continental Europe because they see them as characterless servants of the state. Associated with this, and in spite of a growing hostility to the state and its bureaucratic apparatus, we find an increasing demand that the law integrate itself with the general social machinery for achieving the common good. Law in the Western world, both at the level of judicial process and at the level of legislation, is asked to overcome its abstraction and its underlying individualism, to take into account extra-legal powers and social inequalities, to investigate total social situations, to make orders that will require new powers and new attitudes on the part of courts, to cease treating the 'public interest' as an unruly horse or, at best, as just another private interest to be weighed against the rights of individuals. It is asked instead to recognize a moral hierarchy of interests, to turn its attention from the past actions, immediate interests and abstract rights of the parties before the court to the social context, the social implications and the future consequences of such actions as a general class. Law is being asked to shift its attention from adjudicating between 'private' interests after they are already in conflict to securing and regulating the conduct of social affairs in the name of the social good, and within the adjudicative area to substitute quick *ad hoc* 'justice' for rule-bound 'technicality', the equities of the fireside for legal precept, technique and precedent.

Despite the extent to which these demands carry with them assumptions and criticisms of a clearly socialist colour, they do not come exclusively or even predominantly from consciously socialist groups. The elevation of the direct appeal to public opinion, the weakening of the conceptions of *intra* and *ultra vires*, the rejection of the traditional notion that social institutions have properly limited functions, and a rather new attitude to property and its social role and responsibility, are part of a general social trend. There is a fear of dehumanization in a mass collectivity in which structures have become so vast, the ramifications of technological change so pervasive and irreversible, problems so complex and knowledge so specialized that the individual feels threatened in his ability to cope with, or even to understand, the things that go on around him. His life is changed so immediately and directly, his expectations are transformed at such speed and with such relentlessness that history, technology and 'progress' now appear as enemies rather than friends. Their benefits are assumed, and treated as going on independently of human will or ideology; the demands thay make on human beings are rejected.

There has consequently been a certain retreat from the life and values of enterprise, objective understanding, technical rationality and sustained personal responsibility, with their implied recognition of and respect for external and internal social and physical necessities as frameworks for action. There has been growing disenchantment with those 'rational—legal' modes of life, administration and goal-seeking which Max Weber, and many others, saw as the specific Western contribution to history and civilization. Objectivity has now become, in many quarters, a dirty word, a synonym for the unfeeling and inhuman. The emphasis is on personalization—of administration (evinced by the longing for 'charismatic' leaders), of news reporting, of both popular and intellectual discussion with their gross overvaluing of 'authenticity' and 'commitment', of education (as 'self-expression') and of law. The extreme form of that personalization is the belief that only the sufferer can prescribe the remedy, that only the worm can know the heel, or even more metaphysically that all knowledge is shot through with subjectivity and that only the irrational, inexplicable action is a truly free action.

At a less strident level, much of the revulsion from the individualistic, liberal-democratic concept of the rule of law presents itself as a conscious demand for a return to the face-to-face society, the organic community of living social bonds and commonly shared ideologies and interests. It presents itself, in short, as an elevation of the non-commercial, pre-industrial organic community, the *Gemeinschaft*. Its conceptual opposite, the pluralistic, commercial-individualistic society based on contract, personal responsibility and the rule of law, which the great German sociologist Ferdinand Tönnies called the *Gesellschaft*, is no doubt, as Marxists like to say, in origin a bourgeois phenomenon linked with the ascendancy of cities, trade and manufacture, of internal and external markets, and with the decrease in importance of the agricultural household, kinship, locality and common customs and traditions. That the *Gesellschaft* and its ideology were also a revolt against the bondage of family, status and religion, against the linked personalization and communalization of life, politics and government in the *Gemeinschaft* of feudalism and of traditional pre-industrial societies generally, is now often forgotten. The divorce of law from morality, and of religion from both, the sharp separation of the private and the public, of the legislative, the judicial and the executive, the doctrine of representative government and the abstraction and depersonalization of law and legal administration were charters of liberty without which the character, the achievements and the expectations of modern man would be totally unthinkable. These charters made the American Revolution reverberate throughout Europe, helped to bring down the *ancien régime* and flooded the shores of America with those who left Europe to seek freedom and equality. We cannot understand what the United States meant to nineteenth-century Europe unless we recognize that the movement from status to contract did and does represent a genuine liberation of personality, capacity, thought and opportunity. It is this movement which made socialism and working-class organization possible and which remains the only guarantee of their independent development. It is just such a movement and not any flight back into the *Gemeinschaft* which an increasing number of women are demanding today. If we want to know why, we have only to compare the life, opportunities and expectations of the contemporary American feminist Bella Abzug with those of Nathaniel Hawthorne's heroine, Hester Prynne.

Nevertheless, the liberties of the *Gesellschaft* which have made possible the demands and expectations of modern men and women were gained at a price. That price has been discussed by Karl Marx and by many more recent thinkers, sometimes thoughtfully, sometimes less so, under the heading 'the alienation of man in modern bourgeois (or industrial) society'. The discussion has led to the suggestive, but confused and imprecise contrast, made by members and descendants of the neo-Marxist Frankfurt school like Adorno and Habermas, between *Technik* and *Praxis*, between the requirements of technology, in the widest sense, and the requirements of man—a contrast simplified and vulgarized in the later work of Marcuse. The political liberation of man as a citizen was accompanied (at least in principle) by the liberation of civil society, of the world of industry and trade, from the restraints of religion, morality and politics. Formal political and legal equality concealed and even facilitated real economic and social inequality. Behind the republic of the market lay the despotism of the factory; behind freedom of trade lay the doctrine of the intrinsic social, political, economic and cultural inferiority of colonies and dependencies. For Marx and for less thoughtful Marxists today, these evils flow from private property; for those who think, they are part of a greater and much more complex problem rooted in the technological foundations, organization and scale of modern society.

It is simply true that the ideals and the view of man which

increasingly make gross social and economic inequality, cultural and physical deprivation, despotism and domination morally and politically unacceptable are the very ideals and the view of man brought into history by the *Gesellschaft*—the conception of man as a free moral agent capable of liberty and equality, bound, in his social life, only by laws that he is also capable, as a rational being, of framing, understanding and obeying. It may also be that these are not ideals to be given up lightly even if, like the concept of the juridical person as a free and autonomous agent, they are in actuality fictions. (The alternative, after all, is society as a mental hospital.) Nevertheless, men notice the shoe only where it pinches. *Gesellschaft* law is seen by many in Western societies today as impersonal, inhuman, abstract, itself a form of alienation that tears man out of his living context, fails to see him as a man but recognizes him only as a debtor, a criminal, a ratepayer, a contracting party, in short, as the holder or ower of specific and limited legal rights or duties *vis-à-vis* another, of rights or duties that are external to his personality. There are important reasons connected with the scale of modern economic activity, with the growing power and expanding role of the state and with the attendant bureaucratization of advanced industrial society which make the pure *Gesellschaft* paradigm no longer an effective basis for the legitimation of all fundamental legal and political attitudes in our society or a sufficient source for the organizing concepts on which the whole of our legal and administrative system can be based. But Karl Renner, Max Weber and Josef Schumpeter, who saw these developments clearly, are not the heroes of modern popular and radical ideology, which is much happier talking about 'community' than about the state, about 'participation' than about administration and planning, about 'self-expression' than about emulation. There is that remarkable longing for the personalization of law and legal proceedings, for the restoration of man to a place in the organic community that recognizes him, judges him, and cares for him as a total person, and that makes justice, at least in principle, the work of the whole community and not a specialized branch of learning and experience. There is a parallel enthusiasm for a 'situational ethic' to replace general impersonal principles of conduct. It is here, as one of us has recently stressed,[2] that the admittedly limited appeal of a sentimentalized picture of the People's Republic of China lies. Barefoot doctors seem more human because they are simpler as people, more like ourselves, more accessible than the high priests of a complex and difficult science; in the same way people's courts and people's judges seem more human than the bewigged and gowned representatives of a complex and learned art, which still believes that men must be judged by universal principles grounded in and shaped

[2] A. E. S. Tay, ' "Smash Permanent Rules": China as a Model for the Future', (1976) 7 *Sydney Law Review*, pp. 400–423.

by long-mulled-over and carefully recorded experience and that hard cases make bad law. The sentimentality and superficiality of the new picture is reflected in its comparatively fleeting impact; it is always being undermined by concrete, *real* developments. It is thus that the romantic radical passes, in quick succession, from the achievements and alleged brotherhood of the Soviet Komsomol to Yugoslavia, Cuba, the Congo, China, Chile and even Bangladesh, just as the critics of the medically trained pass from one 'healer' to another.

One basic *motif* in current attitudes, then, is simply the flight, in fantasy, from New York to Marlboro country, from the computers that have replaced the dark Satanic mills to social units where persons still count as persons, with their personal hopes, fears and scars, where they can understand their environment and act upon it, knowing what the effects will be. It is a feeling that has run through the whole history of industrial and post-industrial society, whose dreams and fantasies have always been of a non-industrial, non-specialized and non-fragmented world. Thus Feuerbach abandoned Berlin and Erlangen for Bruckberg, though he lived, like so many drop-outs, off the proceeds of industry, in this case, his wife's share in a porcelain factory. It is a feeling which lies at the very heart of socialism as a historical movement; it has also lain at the very heart of tory conservatism and of the ideologically conservative but practically modernizing fascist right. It is there in the best-selling fiction of the last hundred and fifty years; it is the fantasy that now blatantly dominates our television advertisements; it is reflected in the enthusiasm, among undergraduates of no special ability in any field, for anthropology, prehistory, ecology and the less tough-minded aspects of the biological sciences and for the clothes of eras that will never return and which were at least as nasty, oppressive and cruel as ours.

II

The crisis of liberalism and individualism, of *Gesellschaft* law and of the *Gesellschaft* concept of liberty under law, is the product of great and important changes in modern social and economic life. These point not backward to the *Gemeinschaft*, or forward to the traditional communist utopia, but to a new and much more complex paradigm. Ideologists, however, and popular ideologists above all, see the present in terms of the myths of the past: they go back to old clichés when confronted by new, disturbing and complex developments and thus often help to revitalize them, but at the *expense* of genuine understanding and thought. It is thus that the new developments can be made part of an old, unfulfilled hope. The first, and most superficial, reaction to the current crisis and to demands for participation is to treat them as part of the final, glorious coming of socialism as the enthronement of justice, equality, public interest, the common good and the general will, working to banish injustice, inhumanity and self-seeking individualism from the face of the earth. It is all this which is being suggested, but not spelt out, by shifting discussion from the problem of the relationship of the individual and the state in contractual terms, concerned with rights and duties, to the new language of 'participatory democracy', 'community needs' and 'community development'. This question cannot be looked at seriously without first examining the history of socialism.

The history of socialism can be written as the story of egalitarian strivings, as ancient, perhaps, as society itself; it can be made into the record of the age-old protest against oppression and injustice. As such, it will always be with us; it will have no end. The history of socialism is also part of the history of protest, uprising and revolt, which have their own logic in which popular participation looms large, but only in short-lived transitional periods. In our view the history of socialism is best written and understood not as the history of populism, but as the record of a specific historical development in European society which begins when men bring into relation the political achievements of the French Revolution with the social consequences of the birth of industrial society and the industrial proletariat.[3] The great French Revolution that swept aside the government and law associated with a system of privileges and estates had proclaimed—in one 'world-historical' act of liberation—the slogan 'Liberty, Equality, Fraternity'; it had fixed in an egalitarian universal political constitution the rights of man and of the· citizen. This political liberation, however, as we have said, resulted in a far-reaching economic 'liberation': 'Liberty, Equality, Fraternity' could and did lead to a social order that was profoundly individualistic, weighted in favour of a minority of property owners. As Lichtheim puts it:

> For the bulk of society, then made up of peasants and artisans, economic freedom—in the sense of an uncontrolled market in commodity values, operating in accordance with its own impersonal 'laws'—held danger as much as promise. To the proletariat, already in existence on the eve of the Industrial Revolution in the shape of a mass of paupers deprived of 'active' citizenship, this kind of freedom signified virtually nothing

[3] This is the theme of much of the late George Lichtheim's writing; see especially his *The Origins of Socialism* (New York, 1969), p. 3. In what follows we have drawn on our account of these matters in our 'Beyond the French Revolution: Communist Socialism and the Concept of Law' (1971) 21 *University of Toronto Law Journal*, pp. 109–40, our 'Participation, "Authenticity" and the Contemporary Vision of Man, Law and Society' in R. Cohen, P. K. Feyerabend and M. W. Wartofsky (eds), *Essays in Memory of Imre Lakatos* (Dordrecht, 1976), pp. 561–84 and our 'Socialism, Liberty and Law' in Owen Harries (ed.), *Liberty and Politics: Studies in Social Theory* (London and Sydney, 1976), pp. 81–101.

beyond the bare right to sell one's labour to the highest bidder. Economic liberalism thus conflicted with social democracy, unless it could be shown that all members of society stood an equal chance of attaining to ownership of property. Such an assertion was more plausible in the America of Jefferson and Jackson than in the France of the July Monarchy, or the England of the 1832 Reform Bill, whence the decisive impact of socialist doctrines in Western Europe and their relative failure to attract attention in the United States.[4]

From the disenchantment of the French *sans-culottes* and the radical demands of those who identified with them, from the English social and economic critics of the miseries of the new industrial revolution, from the Saint-Simonian cult of the *industriels*, grew a movement that saw itself as the class ideology of the industrial proletariat. The term 'socialism' made its first appearance in the early 1830s among radical sects in Western Europe. It defined itself through its criticism of bourgeois society, of bourgeois rights and of the economic liberalism associated with these. It brought together, as aspects of one movement, the weavers' revolt in Germany, the abortive 1830 revolution in France and the Chartist agitations in Britain. It fused, or held in loose relation, the Ricardian labour theory of value, the doctrines of Fourier or Saint-Simon and the radical egalitarianism of the extreme democrats of the French Revolution. The link between socialism proper (as the critique of bourgeois society in the light of the Industrial Revolution and of bourgeois civilization's own roots in the Enlightenment) and the prophets, utopians, radical reformers and rebels of earlier days lay in their common hostility to private property, to the inequality of economic position and social opportunity that flowed from the uneven distribution of property and to the power this gave some men over others.

Until the rise of the industrial system, the protest against existing society tended to be a protest against the two most important features of traditional agrarian society—its coercive hierarchy of authority and its distribution (or non-distribution) of property in land. Both these features appeared to be based upon and safeguarded by law. The heroes of socialist prehistory were thus led into inevitable and quite fundamental hostility to law, at least to law as mankind had hitherto known it. The distinguishing mark of the 'progressive' thinker, of the utopian socialist or enlightened democrat, came to be his belief in the intrinsic goodness and sociability of man, or in the view that property was the true source of all significant evils. Not infrequently he saw law, together with private property, as either the cause or the symbol of human misery.

[4] Lichtheim, p.4. America has finally caught up, but the 'demonstration' effect came from blacks and other minorities, backed by the highly ideologized products of the US education system, not from the proletariat.

For Rousseau, natural man, following his spontaneous inclinations, was sociable and benevolent; civilization introduced evil. For Thomas Paine,

> Society is produced by our wants, and government by our wickedness; the former promotes our happiness positively by uniting our affections, the latter negatively by restraining our vices. . . . Government, like dress, is the badge of lost innocence; the palaces of kings are built on the ruins of the bowers of paradise.[5]

Earlier, in 1755, in the Code of Nature at first falsely attributed to Diderot, the utopian 'socialist' or pre-socialist Morelly had written:

> The only vice that I perceive in the universe is *Avarice*; all the others, whatever name they be known by, are only variations, degrees, of this one; it is the Proteus, the Mercury, the basis, the vehicle, of all the vices. Analyse vanity, fatuousness, pride, ambition, duplicity, hypocrisy, dishonesty; break down most of our sophistic virtues into their component parts, and they all resolve themselves into the subtle and pernicious element, *the desire to have* . . .

> Now, would this universal plague, this slow fever, *private interest*, ever have been able to take hold if it had found no sustenance, nor even the slightest dangerous ferment?

> I believe that no one will contest the justness of this proposition: that *where no property exists, none of its pernicious consequences could exist* . . .

> If you were to take away property, and the blind and pitiless self-interest that accompanies it, you would cause all the prejudices and errors that they sustain to collapse. There would be no more resistance, either offensive or defensive, among men; there would be no more furious passions, ferocious actions, notions nor ideas of *moral evil*. If any were to remain, or if some vestige of it were to re-emerge, this would only be the result of the merest accident, one of the smallest consequence. Minor oppositions of will, obfuscating ever so slightly the light of reason among the opponents, would, far from weakening the domination of natural beneficence, only cause men to have a greater sense of its importance . . .[6]

[5] Thomas Paine, *Common Sense and Other Political Writings*, edited by N. F. Adkins (New York, 1953), pp. 54, 55. See also the brilliant discussion of the popular hostility to law in American rural and frontier society between 1800 and 1840 in Perry Miller, *The Life of the Mind in America* (London, 1966), pp. 99–116. Miller describes this hostility as something more than a memory of Tom Paine, as a mood more pervasive than either political party could control, as 'something deep, atavistic, persistent in the community'; p. 103.

[6] Morelly, *Code of Nature*, as translated in Albert Fried and Ronald Sanders, *Socialist Thought: A Documentary History* (Edinburgh, 1964), pp. 18, 19. The classical statement of the contrary view is Mandeville's *Fable of the Bees* (1714), with its insistence that social progress and other *public* benefits depend upon avarice and other *private* vices, though these must, for Mandeville, be placed under some appropriate regulation and restriction.

With the rise of the industrial system, the attack on property gained a new impetus. It was helped by the concentration of the propertyless in the new industrial towns and barracks, but it rested, above all, on the perception that ownership, now of capital and of machines, had, in these new conditions, vastly increased social ramifications. These ramifications stood in direct contradiction to the egalitarian hopes and pretensions of the French Revolution and to the scientific and economic optimism surrounding the Industrial Revolution. The machines that were to make man rich and free were in fact making or keeping thousands poor and dependent. By the late 1820s, some of the followers of Saint-Simon had developed his unflattering contrast between the 'bourgeois' and the '*industriels*' into a far-reaching attack on the role of bourgeois private property in industry. To make the ownership of industrial capital and of the means of production a private concern was *immoral* because it enabled one man to exploit the labour of others; it was *uneconomic* because it failed to provide for the proper planning of industry, for the optimal allocation of resources throughout that vast industrial workshop into which each nation was being turned. Bourgeois society treated property as a private function, when the industrial system was converting it into a social function. The Saint-Simonian Bazard, in the lectures later assembled in the *Exposition* of Saint-Simonian doctrine, was the first to use the phrase 'the exploitation of man by man'; he combined the moral and the economic attacks on private property in the industrial system into a broad indictment:

> If, as we proclaim, mankind is moving toward a state in which all individuals will be classed according to their capacities and remunerated according to their work, it is evident that the right of property, as it exists, must be abolished, because, by giving to a certain class of men the chance to live on the labour of others and in complete idleness, it preserves the exploitation of one part of the population, the most useful one, that which works and produces, in favour of those who only destroy . . .

> [Then] a *social* institution is charged with these functions which today are so badly performed; it is the *depository* of all the instruments of production; it presides over the exploitation of all the material resources; from its vantage point it has a comprehensive view of the whole which enables it to perceive at one and the same time all parts of the industrial workshop . . .

> The social institution of the future will direct all industries in the interest of the whole society, and especially of the peaceful labourers. We call this institution provisionally the general banking system, while entering all reservations against the too narrow interpretation which one might give to this term . . .

The system will include in the first instance a central bank which constitutes the government in the material sphere; this bank will become the
depository of all wealth, of the entire productive fund, of all instruments of
production, in short of everything that today makes up the mass of private
property.[7]

The vital ideological force of Marx's thought lay in his apparent
reconciliation of these two strands—of the vision of the undiffer-
entiated, unstructured community and of the acceptance and
promotion of a planned and industrialized world.

III

The negation or non-recognition of law, N. S. Timasheff has reminded
us,

> may be in the concrete or in the abstract. In the first case the content of law
> is submitted to criticism. The existing legal order, it is felt, should be
> destroyed and replaced by another. This is the usual form of revolu-
> tionary propaganda. It may be successful, but even success would not
> destroy law; only its content would be changed.
>
> In the second case, law as an institution is criticized. Not only should the
> existing legal order be destroyed, but it should be replaced by another
> non-legal order. The triumph of such propaganda would mean the end of
> law as such, and since law is a cultural, historical phenomenon, the
> possibility of its abolition cannot be denied *a priori*.
>
> The abolition of law is the focal point of anarchistic doctrine (in the broad
> sense of the term).[8]

The history of socialism is a complex story. The doctrines that have
been and can be incorporated within the term 'socialism' are not

[7] Celestin Bouglé and Elie Halévy (eds), *Exposition de la doctrine de Saint Simon*
(originally published in 1830 and 1831 by Saint-Simon's disciples), pp. 255, 261, 272–3,
here cited from the translation in Lichtheim, pp. 52–3. Saint-Simon's own use of the
term '*industriels*' combined into a single social class or interest group the industrial
entrepreneur, the scientist and manager and the industrial worker. His disciples in the
1820s were calling for the conversion of private property from an absolute right into a
social function alterable at will; they were not, however, radical egalitarians in the
tradition of Babeuf and his 'Conspiracy of Equals', calling for the total abolition of
property. Their incipient socialist critique of bourgeois society flowered into socialism
in the 1830s. The *Exposition* and Bazard's public lectures familiarized the French public
with the central tenets of the new faith—public ownership and the abolition of social
inequality; *Le Globe*, the journal of the Saint-Simonian Leroux, coined the term
socialisme in February 1832. Marx thought that history had overtaken the Saint-
Simonians, that they were but a prelude to his own truth. He was wrong.

[8] N. S. Timasheff, *An Introduction to the Sociology of Law*, Harvard University
Committee on Research in the Social Sciences (Cambridge, Mass., 1939), p. 367.

mutually consistent and not always internally coherent. They were shaped by men of differing circumstances and temperament, in specific countries and specific historical situations. In France, the extreme democratic wing that emerged from the upheavals of the 1790s stimulated, through Babeuf's follower Buonarroti, the conspiratorial revolutionary socialism of a Blanqui, with its 'dictatorship of true republicans', to be followed by the anarchist and egalitarian communist society. The Paris Commune of 1871 appealed to the 'participatory' tradition of the great Paris Commune of 1793, the commune of Hébert and Chaumette, but it also established a committee of public safety, indicted its own general, and suppressed one newspaper after another, as the Bolsheviks later suppressed the 'maximalists' of Kronstadt and their demand for genuine, elected soviets *after* as well as *before* the assumption of power. In the same France, Saint-Simon and some of his disciples had first looked to their friends in French banking circles to bring about the planning and rationalization of industry and bequeathed to socialism the reformist, state-centred attitudes of a Louis Blanc, attitudes that anticipated the evolutionary democratic socialism that took shape in the 1860s. Fourier's *phalanstères* and Proudhon's rejection of the state stood in direct contradiction to the technocratic ideals of the socialist Saint-Simonians. In England, Robert Owen approached the conclusion of his address to the inhabitants of New Lanark with the words:

> Continue to obey the laws under which you live; and although many of them are founded on principles of the grossest ignorance and folly, yet obey them,—until the government of the country (which I have reason to believe is in the hands of men well disposed to adopt a system of general improvement) shall find it practicable to withdraw those laws which are productive of evil, and introduce others of an opposite tendency.[9]

Only fourteen years later, however, in conjunction with the agitation for the Great Charter, the 'hewers of wood and the drawers of water' in England were demanding to know in what way the Reform Bill could benefit them and were expressing their lack of faith in the country's laws and institutions in a wave of violent protest.

Socialism may thus be revolutionary or evolutionary, anarchist or étatist. Whether its criticism of law is—in Timasheff's terms— 'concrete' or 'abstract', a criticism of a particular legal system or of law in general, is not always clear. Certainly, as a movement of (or on behalf of) the deprived and the oppressed, socialism of all types reflected the latter's intense antagonism to the existing state and the existing system, and for those who seemed to know how to manipulate the rules of the system to their own advantage. The French Revolution

---

[9] Fried and Sanders, p. 183.

had swept away the trappings (if not the entire core) of the centuries-old legal traditions of the *ancien régime*, with their estates, privileges and feudal dues, and had enacted a series of constitutions followed by a code that was to be the glory of modern Europe. Socialists stood in a relation of radical criticism to the rights of the citizen and the civil and political arrangements embodied in these constitutions and this code. They rejected not only 'feudal' law, but 'bourgeois' law as well. Was their rejection of bourgeois law, then, 'concrete' or 'abstract'?

The Rousseauan-anarchist tradition in socialism gave a clear answer to this question. It believed in the fundamental and natural cooperativeness of men, in the triumph of reason and of the general will. In a truly human society, there would be no need for a coercive state and a system of law. In a speech to the German Workers' Educational Association in London, in June 1845, the quasi-religious German communist Wilhelm Weitling declared: 'In my opinion, everyone is ripe for communism, even the criminals. Criminals are a product of the present order of society, and under communism they would cease to be criminals. Humanity is of necessity always ripe for revolution, or it never will be.'[10] The anarcho-communism of which Weitling was a simple-minded exponent was to find its place in the infinitely more sophisticated Marxian system—though only as long as it remained in opposition, not when it governed.

If the anarchists and anarcho-communists clearly rejected law in the abstract, the connection between this rejection and socialism as the critique of bourgeois society remained unclear. Proudhon's famous slogan 'Property is theft' implied—as Marx was clear to note—that concept of property which Proudhon was claiming to expose, for theft is the taking of something that 'belongs' to another.[11] Was the abolition of property to be followed by legislation, creating a new legal system for a socialist society? Morelly's attack on property and the desire for property was supplemented by an elaborate model code—the Code of Nature—with its sacred and fundamental laws, distributive or economic laws, agrarian laws, edile laws, police laws, sumptuary laws and so on. The étatist socialists clearly thought in terms of state regulation that would direct and control the material foundations and social life of a socialist society. Yet socialism, as Dicey's discussion of 'collectivism' notes, did not come upon the world with a distinctive socialist theory of law and in England (and elsewhere) it has never attained to one. The early socialists, no doubt, had their attention

[10] Cited in Boris Nicolaevsky and Otto Maenchen-Helfen, *Karl Marx: Man and Fighter* (London, 1936), pp. 113–14.

[11] Proudhon himself was not guilty of contradiction; he made it clear that the 'property' he was denouncing as theft was property in the means of production and the labour of others, not property in general. This is now the position of all communist parties and governments, though the Chinese avoid the commonly used term 'personal' or 'individual' property.

engaged by other matters, economics and the problem of smashing or gaining state power. As revolutionaries they naturally provided no blue-print for the future, as evolutionary reformers they worked within an existing system. There was, however, a fundamental ambiguity in the pre-Marxian socialist relation to law that cuts deeper than this. Socialists saw the existing legal system, and all major legal systems before it, as involving, in a fundamental and pervasive way, the concept of property and of individual rights as opposed to social responsibilities. When the concept of property and of the independent self-contained individual was excised from law, as from social life, what would remain? Some veered to the view that the new order would be based on new social customs and habits rather than on formal indictments and the possibility of formal litigation. Courts would give way to assemblies. Others, like Morelly, saw the new society as based on a complex and pervasive set of *regulations*, administrative arrangements that defined duties, allocated resources and conferred or denied material and political rights, but which converted all legal problems and disputes into matters for administrative and political decision. It is a problem that Marx did *not* solve, even if anyone who studies the history of socialism in the twentieth century knows which view has triumphed, and which has remained in permanent opposition. What Marx did was to shirk the problem by seeing the revolution and its immediate aftermath as centralized and coercive, and relegating the anarchist component to a future stage of true Communism that has receded further and further into the future.

IV

The classical Marxist theory of state and law is reasonably well known. From the *German Ideology* onwards, Marx (and Engels) saw the state as by its essence a coercive organ of class domination imposing the will of the ruling class on the rest of society and using law and legal enactments as sanctioned expressions of that will. When antagonistic classes disappear, when there is no longer a ruling class, the state and law necessarily wither away, to be replaced by the moral consciousness and general will of the community and by communist self-administration. This withering away of state and law, Marx and Engels made clear, required, and presupposed, the overcoming of the division of labour and the abolition of any specific bureaucratic or managerial or political caste that made representing the social interest a sectional or particular interest. The disappearance of the state, in other words, required not only the abolition of classes, but the overcoming of alienation.

In the *Critique of the Gotha Programme* and in one or two other places, Marx referred to the fact that the proletarian revolution would be a seizure of state power and that the revolution would be followed by a dictatorship of the proletariat. The proletariat, as the *Communist Manifesto* put it, 'will use its political supremacy to wrest by degrees all capital from the bourgeoisie, to centralize all instruments of production in the hands of the state, i.e., of the proletariat organized as the ruling class', and to suppress the remnants of earlier ruling classes seeking to undo the work of the revolution and to topple the rule of the majority. Thus Engels stresses that 'the first act in which the state genuinely comes forward as the representative of society as a whole—the taking possession of the means of production in the name of society—is at the same time its last independent act as a state. The interference of state power in social relations becomes superfluous in one sphere after another and then ceases of itself. The government of persons is replaced by the administration of things and the direction of the process of production. The state is not abolished, it withers away.'

In *State and Revolution* and in his much quoted lecture on the state at Sverdlov University, Lenin unreservedly accepted this view, that the state is based on class division, that it is in essence organized violence and that the dictatorship of the proletariat creates a state that is so constituted that it begins to wither away immediately and cannot help but wither away. Revolutionary politics may use the forms of state and law but only as a *means*. It creates conditions in which they will completely disappear.

The tension between this view of the matter and Lenin's very considerable use of state power, including bureaucratic machinery and legislative decrees and the suppression of soviets and independent working-class representation, was glossed over by the feeling that the latter were all rapidly changing means to an end, that state and law were no more than tools in the process of revolutionary transformation. The period of 'war communism' from 1918 to 1921, like the early years of the Chinese People's Republic, saw the emphasizing of the *Gemeinschaft* concept of revolutionary justice, based on informal popular procedures and on the intense politicalization of such law and administration as were found necessary, mixing these with the deliberate use of terror as an instrument of social policy. Then, suddenly, the Soviet government proclaimed its New Economic Policy, encouraging state-controlled capitalist development. It promulgated, from 1922 onward, a whole series of formal codes of law and procedure, which borrowed freely from the 'bourgeois' codes of the Continent, and laid the foundations of what was later called 'socialist law'. The withering away of state and law, seen as imminent during the period of 'war communism', was now pushed further into the future, while the administrative trends inherent in the New Economic Policy were brought to their fullest economic development with the abolition, in 1927, of the NEP's licensed capitalism and the inauguration of the two five-year plans, spanning the period from 1928 to 1936. The dominant attitude among the party ideologists of the time was that expressed somewhat later by the leading Marxist jurisprudential thinker, E. B. Pashukanis. He insisted that law was in its very essence a market phenomenon, representing the maximum stability, immobility of framework required by bourgeois commercial relations; it was in flat contradiction to the needs of the proletarian revolution, which demanded maximum flexibility for the rapid transformation of the whole of society and which elevated socio-economic norms and community interests above the abstract legal rights and duties of individual juridical subjects.[12] The famous *ABC of Communism* prepared by N. Bukharin and E. Preobrazhenski in 1919 as a commentary on and an exposition of the communist programme adopted at the eighth party congress had—quite typically—devoted six of its 424 pages to law, under the title 'Proletarian Justice'.

True, while Lenin feared and to some extent struggled against a bureaucratization of a state apparatus, while he insisted that Soviet laws were means of propaganda rather than administration, and while Pashukanis and A. G. Goikhbarg insisted that there was no such thing as a socialist system of law, other voices stressed the need for regular procedures, consistent court decisions, and administrative regularity.[13] These voices represented the continuity of bureaucratic, administrative and, to some extent, middle-class values within the revolution; and they were given a certain added strength and point by the requirements of the New Economic Policy as well as by the exigencies of centralized planning. The vast majority of the professional cadres in the 1920s were not Bolsheviks, but professionals with a sense of the requirements of their subject, socialists or social

---

[12] See E. B. Pashukanis, *Obshchaya teoriya prava i Marksizm* (*The General Theory of Law and Marxism*, Moscow, 1924), and his address to a congress of Soviet lawyers in Moscow in 1930, both translated into English in Hugh W. Babb and John N. Hazard, *Soviet Legal Philosophy* (Cambridge, Mass., 1951), pp. 111ff.

[13] Since 1936, and especially since the promulgation of the new civil and criminal codes in the period 1958–64, there has been a steady rewriting of the history of Soviet law which verges on falsification. The 1922 codes are no longer treated as necessary concessions flowing from the NEP and the transitional requirements of the dictatorship of the proletariat, but as the foundations of a new system of Soviet socialist law. Thus, in K. A. Sofronenko (ed.), *Istoriya gosudarstva i prava SSSR* (*History of the Government and Law of the USSR* Moscow, 1962), II, at p. 160, O. I. Chistyakov claims that the primary reason for the promulgation of codes in 1922–3 was the accumulation of decisions by people's courts needing systematization and embodiment in a code to ensure that they would be accessible to lawyers. The aim of the codes, he says, was to strengthen socialist legality and the people who opposed such codification are branded by him as 'opportunists'; the fact that the entire Soviet leadership of the period agreed in seeing a codified legal system as transitional is simply ignored.

democratic Marxists rather than Leninists. The lawyers and even the judges in their daily work (with good reason) were not happy about an undefined revolutionary consciousness of justice or about the notion that socialism meant the overcoming of all law. Neither were the peasants. The Pashukanis theory that law was based on the equivalence and atomization of juridical subjects and was therefore a typical commercial, bourgeois phenomenon unsuited to socialism was by far the most radical view, even among Marxists. A. Ya Vyshinsky, in his great denunciation in 1938 of the 'traitors and wreckers' Krylenko, Pashukanis and Stuchka, helped to obscure the very real differences between their positions. Even Pashukanis himself was no simple-minded anarchist thinking that socialist society would simply run itself *á la* Lenin's *State and Revolution*. For him the distinguishing mark of socialism was the fact that it was not governed by law, but by socio-technical norms, by the rational requirements of a rational process of production. Such norms, for Pashukanis, created a (complex, but non-legal) system of *administration*, emphasizing vertical relations of direction and subordination, and thus distinguished from a system of law, emphasizing horizontal relations between equivalent right-and-duty-bearing individuals or legal personalities. For Stuchka, for a period president of the Supreme Court of the RSFSR and more deeply immersed in practical legal work than Pashukanis, the norms involved in the process of production were legal and therefore, until such norms were internalized by workers, there was a socialist system of law. Nevertheless, in the period 1917–28, at least formally, the collective and the proletariat were always elevated above state and law, while the succeeding period of the five-year plans from 1928 to 1936 elevated plan above state, law and the (empirical, existing) proletariat. If the state was not actively withering away, it was certainly not being elevated as an independent and important social category in the Soviet Union, and at least some legal theorists looked forward to the day when the Institute of Soviet Construction and Law could simply be called the Institute of Soviet Construction.

It is perhaps not easy to speak quite as confidently of the period 1929 to 1936 as of the period 1921 to 1928. The shifts in Soviet ideology have not been quite as sharp and unexpected as earlier Western observers often thought them. What appeared to be the startling reversal of 1936, the denunciation of Stuchka and Pashukanis for their anti-Marxist theory of the withering away of law in the period of socialist construction, was in fact preceded by mounting criticism of Pashukanis's theories from 1929 onwards, accompanied by several significant recantations by Pashukanis himself. Nevertheless, throughout this later period the Soviet state was still represented as embodying or manifesting the dictatorship of the proletariat, and there was no emphasis on its independent creative role. It was essentially a coercive organ embodying the will of the dominant class, thereby and only thereby did it belong to the general genus 'state'. Its economic, cultural and administrative functions, while recognized, were all exercised on behalf of the proletariat and not as typical or essential state functions. If the state still existed, then, it was only because the dictatorship of a single class had not yet ended. The will of the proletariat—though already the will of the majority of the Soviet people, indeed of mankind—had still to be imposed on the whole Soviet society and defended against internal and external enemies. Then, in 1936, Stalin proclaimed that the Soviet Union had entered upon socialism, and that there were now only non-antagonistic classes in the Soviet Union. Nevertheless, the state was not to disappear and law was not to begin withering away. On the contrary, they were to enter upon a new creative period. Indeed, the Institute of Soviet Construction and Law, instead of being renamed the Institute of Soviet Construction, became in 1938—when Vyshinsky ousted Pashukanis as director—the Institute of State and Law. The main basis of the continued existence of the Soviet state was still seen as lying in the need for dictatorship, but this was now based on the external hostility with which the homeland of socialism was confronted. (Internal wreckers and saboteurs, while still given prominence in propaganda, were now seen at the theoretical level as primarily agents of external interests or as unreconstructed criminals without a social base and not as bearers of unliquidated pre-revolutionary interests and classes.) In 1940, Stalin wrote of this period:

> The function of military suppression inside the country ceased, died away, for exploitation had been abolished, there were no more exploiters left, and so there was no one to suppress. In place of this function of suppression, the state acquired the function of protecting socialist property from thieves and pilferers of the people's property. The function of defending the country from foreign attack fully remained: consequently the Red Army and the navy fully remained, as did the punitive organs and the intelligence service, which are indispensable for the detection and punishment of the spies, assassins and wreckers sent to our country by foreign espionage services. The function of economic organization and cultural education by the state organs also remained, and was developed to the full. Now the main task of our state inside the country is the work of peaceful economic organization and cultural education. As for our army, punitive organs and intelligence service, their edge is no longer turned to the inside of the country but to the outside, against external enemies.[14]

This new emphasis on the peaceful but creative role of the Soviet

[14] Stalin, *Report to the Eighteenth Congress of the CPSU* (1939). He was lying.

state—though it could be backed with earlier references to the might and importance of the organs of the revolutionary proletariat organized as a state—was nevertheless a very real and sharp shift in official theory. It was justified by Stalin by an appeal to Hegelian philosophy. The state as a historical category could be transcended and abolished (*aufgehoben*) only after the potentialities of that category had been developed and exhausted to the full. The socialist state, though a transitional state, must therefore first become the strongest and most perfect state in history; only then would it begin to wither away. Thus, the state was elevated into a fundamental and principal category in Soviet society. Paeans of praise were now sung to the perfection of the Soviet state[15] and to Soviet law as the most truly legal of all legal systems, as a mighty force in protecting the interests of the people and of socialism.

This elevation of the Soviet state into a fundamental social category required some very major emendations to classical Marxist theory. The state and law were clearly part of the superstructure. Historical materialism, therefore, had to be reinterpreted (with the aid of long-familiar texts from Engels) to say that the superstructure could react back on the base and become a mighty force in aiding the material transformation of the base. This was done in Stalin's well-known philosophical contribution to *The History of the CPSU—A Short Course* in 1938, consolidated and extended in his *Marxism and Questions of Linguistics* in 1950.

What all this led to in practice was characterized accurately enough by Yugoslav communists after their break with Stalin in 1949. In the Soviet Union, the Yugoslav party theorist Eduard Kardelj wrote,

> The state, or the party apparatus—which are one and the same thing— have become a totally independent power above the people. Thus the state in the Soviet Union and in the lands with Cominform governments is not a state in the Marxist or Leninist sense, namely a state which is so organized that it can gradually wither away. On the contrary, in the Soviet Union a theory has been evolved that the state must be strengthened in all its functions, in order that, in this way alone, the conditions should be created for the 'commencement' of the state's withering away. . . . In the whole history of humanity there has never existed a state which was to such a degree centralized, and which was such an overweening factor in the life of the people, as this state is.[16]

On the theoretical side, however, there were already signs of the

---

[15] See, for example, P. F. Yudin, *O sovetskom sotsialisticheskom obshchestve* (*On Soviet Socialist Society*, Moscow, 1949), p. 22, cited by Ivo Lapenna, *State and Law: Soviet and Yugoslav Theory* (London, 1964), pp. 39–40.

[16] Kardelj, *Deset Godina Narodne Revolucije* (*Ten Years of People's Revolution*, Belgrade, 1951), p. 63, translated by Lapenna, p. 45.

tensions in Marxist theory of state and law that were to become all too evident in the post-Stalin period. Officially, during the whole period from 1936 to the death of Stalin, the state, despite its peaceful organizing and educative functions, was defined as in essence a coercive instrument. Its *sine qua non* was still seen as lying in the need for suppression and defence. The continued existence of the state was therefore now tied quite specifically to the danger of capitalist encirclement and penetration. Engels's formula concerning the withering away of the state was specifically declared to be inapplicable to socialism in a single country because the continued existence of capitalism required the strengthening of organized force and vigilance. The state will be preserved, even under communism, Malenkov wrote in his report to the nineteenth congress of the CPSU in 1952, if capitalist encirclement still remained.

The same was true of law. Throughout this period, law was defined as the totality of norms, or rules, of conduct strengthening the domination of one class, expressing its will and ensuring the existence of social relations congenial or advantageous to it. The emphasis was on law as state-sanctioned will. The official dominant line was no doubt strengthened even further by the conditions that obtained in the decade and a half after 1936—the purges, the War and the Cold War, all leading to a natural emphasis on the repressive and defensive powers of the state and on law as criminal law. Nevertheless, the new Stalinist doctrine of the state and of the importance of socialist legality, to some extent, pulled in the opposite direction. The emphasis of the creative role of the state at least laid the foundations for considering, more seriously than Marxist ideologists had hitherto done, the organizational, technical and specialized functions of the state. The Stalin Constitution, with its at any rate theoretical protection, within limits, of such specific categories as interests and rights of the individual, of the family and of personal property, reaffirmed the complexity and the comparative plurality of interests against the monolithic mobilizational concerns of Plan. Where Pashukanis had looked forward to adjudication between interests being replaced by administration and the application of socio-technical norms, the Stalin Constitution, at least formally, elevated the adjudicative *Gesellschaft* view of law and the continuation of civil law relations, presupposing discrete interests in a socialist society.[17] The legal texts of this period

[17] A few years ago, when I spent some months going in very careful detail through virtually all published Soviet writing on the law of tort and questions of liability for personal injuries, I was rather surprised to find that the growth of a professional body of technical and detailed legal literature in this area went back to 1940 and not to 1953. One did not feel that the leading civil law writers of the Stalinist period—Agarkov, Fleishits and Antimonov, for instance—were mere ideological hacks, or that the books they wrote in the Stalinist period were significantly less professional and intelligent than the widely

7

recognized that law had an intricate and complex content, but the complexity is still shorn of any ultimate independence or of any ultimate significance for a theory of the state and social administration by this reduction of the content of law to that of morality. In this way, the doctrine that law in a socialist society had no special intrinsic character or grounds for existence was still maintained. Socialist law was embryonic communist morality and proletarian interest backed by state sanction; it was not an independent system or way of looking at things.

The history of any society is not a monolithic story, however much its rulers wish it were. The Soviet state, communist jurists have stressed, 'emerged not on the basis of some written statutes, but as a result of the direct initiative of the masses, which in the course of the revolution destroyed the old order, the old legality, the old system of authorities, and created in their stead their own system of power, their own governmental agencies'.[18] If we substitute Lenin and the Bolshevik Party organization for 'the masses', this account is substantially correct. The power of the Soviet state rested, and substantially still rests, on extra-legal relations of domination and submission. The relation of domination and submission is extra-legal and supra-legal in that it neither implies nor requires a structured system of regulation incorporating certain values and moral or socio-political assumptions; gangsters can and do rule by terror and the imposition of force; communist regimes have been very quick to take this point and to apply it in practice. Nevertheless, in communist countries generally, and in the Soviet Union initially, the domination-submission relationship has been both institutionalized and ideologized in the doctrine of the leading role and historical infallibility of the Communist Party and in the proclamation of 'democratic centralism' or, in practice, of unquestioning obedience to decisions from above. A vast range of legal and extra-legal measures have been taken to ensure that domination remains secure. The economic and administrative arrangements of the Soviet Union, the role of the state as the only significant employer and the complex and efficient system of political controls preventing the formation of

published, 'liberal' civil law texts of the post-Stalin period. (What is true is that the Soviet legal journals were unreadable in the 1940s and early 1950s whereas they have become steadily more readable since.) In the really professional leading monograph literature on technical problems of law, there is less discontinuity between the Stalinist and the post-Stalinist period than one might have expected. Nevertheless, the uncomfortable implications for Marxism of this growing professionalization of law after 1936 were successfully glossed over by treating the conceptual content of law as fundamentally ideological and educative, by reducing the content of law to that of morality. (A.E.S.T.)

[18] *Sorok let sovetskogo prava 1917–1957* (*Forty Years of Soviet Law 1917–1957*, Moscow, 1957), 1, p. 16.

independent power bases are the primary source of Soviet communist domination. Nevertheless, the development of the Soviet Union has seen sharp tensions between three types of social and administrative ideology implicit in Marxism and in the social situation of a country going through accelerated industrialization and modernization. The *Gemeinschaft* ideology and view of law, linked with the utopian-anarchist component in Marxism and drawing to some extent on the traditions of the peasant *mir*, rejects legalistic and bureaucratic methods of control and relies on spontaneous, informal community pressure, 'revolutionary justice' and social opinion. This strain puts a heavy premium on conformity, in principle rejects completely legal safeguards that would protect the individual from social persecution and provides, in both Soviet and Chinese conditions, forms of social pressure that are hard to resist and are yet almost completely open to manipulation by the party and the authorities. It has also from time to time enabled the regime to turn to its own use popular anti-semitism, dislike of intellectuals and resentment of dissident nationalisms by allowing popular prejudice to claim the right to be heard, even in formal legal proceedings.

A second strain, the administrative-bureaucratic strain, sees law as concerned with social regulation in terms of the state and party interests and not as adjudication between private or individual interests. It is the strongest strain in the Soviet Union; it is entrenched in various ways in the civil and criminal codes, which see all rights as *granted by the state* and wrongs as those activities which are *socially* dangerous. It accounts for the concern, in Soviet administration and Soviet legal proceedings, with a kind of bureaucratic correctness and pedantry. Soviet courts will ride blatantly over constitutional and individual rights; but they are genuinely shocked if the file is not in order, if the proper bureaucratic preliminaries to the trial have not been carried out in proper bureaucratic form.

The third strain, the *Gesellschaft* strain, stems, curiously enough, from the emphasis on socialist legality, impartial arbitration and formal constitutions beginning with the New Economic Policy and strengthened during the period of Stalin, mostly with an eye on internal stability and foreign propaganda. It involves at least lip-service to constitutionality, independence of the judiciary, formal legal correctness, and the protection, even if in a very, very limited way, of individual rights and some civil liberties. The death of Stalin, which allowed these strains and the tensions between them to come more openly to the surface, also seemed—at first sight—to involve a considerable strengthening of the *Gesellschaft* strain in Soviet administration and law, an increased concern with legal rights and procedural guarantees as safeguards against the abuse of power. Khrushchev's secret speech about the abuses of the cult of personality

F

at the twentieth party congress in 1956, the new codes of law and procedure enacted from 1958 onward and the frank discussion of Stalin's 'illegalities' at the twenty-second party congress in 1961—in brief, all those Soviet developments that the Chinese have abused as 'modern revisionism'—encouraged or responded to an increasing concern with *Gesellschaft* ideology in the Soviet Union. This concern was in part linked, no doubt, with the bureaucratic-administrative interest in predictability, stability and the precise definition of jurisdictional and administrative competence. It stood in sharp contradiction to the *ad hoc* procedures and uncertainties of the *Gemeinschaft* strain.

In fact, however, Khrushchev was not only far from creating a *Rechtsstaat*; he was far from committing himself or the CPSU to a particular trend among these three. He was making an imaginative and creative bid to hold these mutually antagonistic conceptions together, while giving a new impetus (and a restricted function) to each. At the twenty-second party congress in 1961, it was announced that the period of the dictatorship of the proletariat had ended, that the Soviet state was a 'State of the Entire People' and that the Soviet Union had now entered into the period of the accelerated building of communism in which state and law might be expected to wither away; on the face of it this proclaimed that the *Critique of the Gotha Programme* and Lenin's *State and Revolution* were still sound guideposts to the development of Soviet society. In fact, it required a major reappraisal of the Marxist theory of state and law. The Stalinist view that the complete withering away of the state required an internal condition, the building of a developed communist society, and an external condition, the victory and consolidation of socialism in the world arena, was still specifically reaffirmed in the party programme adopted at the twenty-second congress. But the dictatorship of the proletariat ended before the state withered away; therefore the state could no longer be defined in the traditional way as the coercive organ of class rule. Writing in *Kommunist* in 1961 (no. 13, p. 44), F. Burlatsky emphasized that the classical definition of the state as an instrument of the ruling class no longer applies to the *Soviet* state, which has ceased to be an instrument of class domination and has become an instrument of society as a whole: 'The socialist state is an agency of the power of the whole people, an instrument by means of which society builds communism, safeguards the rights and freedoms of citizens, the socialist legal order and socialist property, ensures defence and maintains normal reciprocal relations with other countries.'

The programme of the CPSU adopted at the twenty-second party congress says:

> The party holds that the dictatorship of the working class ceases to be neccessary before the state withers away. The state as an all-people's

organization will survive until the full victory of communism. Expressing the will of the people, it is called upon to organize the building up of the material-technical basis of communism, the transformation of socialist relations into communist relations, to exercise control over the measure of work and measure of consumption, to promote the well-being of the people, to safeguard the rights and freedoms of Soviet citizens, the socialist legal order and socialist property, to educate the masses of people in the spirit of conscious discipline and of a communist attitude to labour, reliably to ensure the defence and security of the country, to develop fraternal cooperation with the socialist countries, to uphold the cause of world peace and to maintain normal relations with all countries.

Where Stalin had seen the strengthening of the state as a necessary precondition for its withering away, Khrushchev had proclaimed (to the twenty-first party congress in 1959) that the question should be treated 'dialectically'—the strengthening of the state and its withering away could be to some extent simultaneous. Certainly, he said, the transformation of the socialist state into communist self-adminis-tration had now been put on the agenda of the state function itself by the new phase of the accelerated building of communism (that is, now, if not earlier, the Soviet state did have the function of entering immediately upon the task of abolishing itself).

The effect of all this was to direct new attention to the complexity of state functions, to the fact that they were not all of one piece and that the relationship between present state functions and future communist self-administration was rather more complex than suggested in Lenin's *State and Revolution,* where every cook became a politician and where economic planning became the concern of everyone who knew that two and two make four. Writers began to emphasize that authority relations would not simply disappear under communism and that specialized functions and skills would still, at least to some extent, remain. They now recalled Engels's famous letter to some Italian anarchists who had questioned the Marxist emphasis on industrial discipline, in which Engels wrote:

> At least with regard to the hours of work one may write upon the portals of these factories: '*Lasciate ogni autonomia, voi che entrate!*' [Leave, ye that enter, all autonomy behind!] If man, by dint of his knowledge and inventive genius, has subdued the forces of nature, the latter avenge themselves upon him by subjecting him, in so far as he employs them, to a veritable despotism, independent of all social organization. Wanting to abolish all authority in large-scale industry is tantamount to wanting to abolish industry itself, to destroy the power loom in order to return to the spinning wheel.[19]

[19] As cited in Marx and Engels, *Basic Writings on Politics and Philosophy*, edited by Lewis S. Feuer (New York, 1963), p. 483.

The leading 'official' Soviet theoretician of state and law, P. S. Romashkin, developed this theme:

> [Self-governing associations in communist] society will be established with a maximum amount of democracy—periodic changes in personnel, composition, subject to control by the people, etc., and, most important of all, the personnel of the apparatus of public self-government will not constitute a profession of 'administrators'. . . . Basic functions of the socialist state—those of management of the economy and culture, upbringing and education, distribution of labour and consumption— will not disappear but will be transformed in accordance with the development of society. The bodies involved in planning and accounting, in directing the economy and culture, which are now state bodies, will gradually lose their political character, and the whole population will be drawn into this work both through the public organization and directly.
>
> The principle of universal participation of the masses in administration under communism will not mean an anarchic changing of occupations and forms of activity, an unsystematic involvement of citizens in public administration, since this contradicts the very character of highly organized production. Two fundamental conclusions follow from this. First, citizens will participate in the work of the various public administrative bodies, including the representative bodies, in accordance with their professional interests and knowledge. Second, the universal character of the involvement of the masses does not apparently preclude the possibility of certain persons being occupied, along with other work, in exercising the functions of technical administration—planning, accounting, distribution, etc.—and ensuring the continuing of the performance of these functions. We refer to a special group of highly experienced specialists who can ensure daily fulfilment of duties in the organization of social production.
>
> Consequently, the process of the withering away of law, if understood dialectically, is one of the development of socialist law into non-legal communist rules of behaviour which do not require any special apparatus of state coercion. It would of course be wrong to put the matter so simply that communist rules of behaviour will have nothing in common with the present legal norms. On the contrary, they will develop not only out of the legal norms which exist today but also to a significant extent out of the moral and other social norms of socialist society, and will absorb all that is best from both with respect to their inner content and form. But rules established today in the form of legal norms will occupy an important place among them. These rules, having lost their juridical nature, will become a part of the system of social norms of the future communist society. In content they will be the same in many cases as the requirements, rules and prescriptions of the existing juridical norms, with this difference, that they will no longer have a juridical character. The communist norms may in form be like the legal norms now in force (written norms, moral codes and so on).[20]

[20] P. S. Romashkin, 'Voprosy razvitiya gosudarstva i prava v proekte Programmy KPSS' ('Problems of the Development of State and Law in the Draft Programme of the CPSU'), (1961) *Sovetskoe gosudarstvo i pravo*, no. 10, p. 26.

On the legal side, very considerable tensions emerged in the freer legal discussions of the late 1950s and early 1960s, during which an adjudicative concept of justice and an interest in formal procedure and substantive guarantees were espoused by a number of 'liberal' legal theorists. The comparative de-ideologization of professional disciplines and the attack on Stalin's and Vyshinsky's abuses of judicial process and violations of legal norms did lead to such a marked emphasis, among liberal Soviet writers, on the merit and social significance of legal attitudes and forms. This came to the verge of seeing the essence of law in a formal concept of justice, but did stop short of entering on that very subversive territory. No 'licensed' theoretician in the Soviet Union is yet prepared to say, or able to say, that law is justice and that justice has its own requirements, whether these be seen as purely procedural or substantive. A closer approach to this has been made in recent work on civil law by N. S. Bratus and O. S. Ioffe. Obviously influenced by the previously condemned work of Pashukanis, they defined civil law relations as being distinguished from administrative relations by their emphasis on equivalence and equality and as being expressions of relationships in a commodity-exchanging, monetary society. Civil law will thus exist so long as money exists.

The fall of Khrushchev from power has not led to a repudiation of the concept that the Soviet state is a state of all the people and not a class dictatorship. One Soviet writer has stressed that penal sanctions and the criminal law are no longer matters involving the concept of class: criminals, he argues, do not constitute a class in Soviet society; individual parasitic elements, he says, do not constitute a class.[21] The new codes of law in the Soviet Union, and this includes the All-Union Criminal *Osnovy* (Fundamental Principles) and the Republican Codes of 1956-60, do not refer—as the codes of the 1920s did—to class interest, or to the concepts of class origin, class affiliation and 'enemy of the people', which have been formally excised from the law. Neither has Khrushchev's fall led to any formal repudiation of his widely publicized doctrine that the Soviet Union has now entered upon the accelerated building of communism and that state and law will therefore begin, selectively, to wither away. The boasts about the speed with which Russia will reach communism have ceased. The concept of 'withering away' has been given a rather technical meaning that is perhaps too subtle for Khrushchev himself (whose model of future Soviet social development strove to marry Yugoslav and Chinese elements). The theoretical writing since Khrushchev's fall,

---

[21] A. Butenko, 'Sovetskoe obshchenarodnoe gosudarstvo' ('The Soviet All-People's State') in *Kommunist* (1963), no. 13, 22 at pp. 31 and 32; translated as 'The Soviet State of the Entire People' in (1963/4) 2 *Soviet Law and Government*, no. 3, 3 at p. 12.

especially after the hardening treatment of 'liberals' that set in from 1966 onwards, suggests a return to caution in place of Khrushchev's notorious boldness, a greater emphasis on social and theoretical complexity and a temporary stalemate between certain fundamental tensions or trends in Soviet society, together with a greater willingness to treat even Soviet and socialist society in a more detailed historical perspective, requiring different legal and constitutional arrangements at different periods of development. The tension between the *Gemeinschaft* interest in informal, 'popular' tribunals that judge the whole man in the concrete social situation in which he finds himself, the *Gesellschaft* conception of law as precise, predictable and operating according to its own specific, judicial conceptions, and the bureaucratic-administrative concern with organization, administration and direction is now quite open, even if Soviet theorists cannot put matters in this way. Thus, while some of the ideologists talk about the educative function of law and the way in which law will pass over into moral and social norms supported by popular sentiment rather than state sanctions, the legal journals call for more detailed and more technical legal research, for a deeper appreciation of the complexities involved in the legal structure and regulation of society and even for a more systematic and worked-out definition of the powers and constitutional functions of higher organs of government. Even the ideologists, commissioned to rebut the theory of the Cultural Revolution in China, have begun to explain openly that the abolition of the division of labour does not mean the abolition of a division of functions or that fully-developed communism can do without professional experts whose skills will be much too specialized and too hard to attain to be generally spread throughout the community. Thus Yu. A. Tikhomirov, in an article entitled 'Division of Powers or Division of Labour?',[22] argues that to single out a special group of persons to exercise the functions of state powers is not to create a social stratum but merely to create 'a portion of the labouring population that has been given shape in an organizational and legal sense'. He distinguishes three forms of participation in power—the direct, the representative and the professional. All three, he makes it clear, will always be with us, though more recent Soviet work, in the general spirit of the times and to offset the increasingly naked bureaucratization of the Soviet leadership, emphasizes the continuities between state and society and the social character of future state constitutions, which will also be constitutions of society—

[22] Published as 'Razdelenie vlastei ili razdelenie truda' in (1967) *Sovetskoe gosudarstvo i pravo*, no. 1, p.14; translated in (1967) 5 *Soviet Law and Government* no. 2 See also Yu. A. Tikhomirov, '*Vlast*', *demokratiya, professionalizm*' ('State Power, Democracy, Professionalism'), (1968) *Sovetskoe gosudarstvo i pravo*, no. 1, p. 24.

in other words, provide for the institutionalization of 'social' organizations and groupings.[23]

V

The central problems of socialism have changed remarkably little, even if the world has changed far more. The Marxian synthesis, a tremendous act of force and faith, has once again come apart to reveal its disparate components. The talk is of private interest giving way to 'the social interest', of the values and ideals enshrined in Roman and common law giving way to the values and ideals of 'society', especially of 'contemporary society'. But the central contradiction of socialism, or, at least, the central tension within it, lies precisely in its attempt to give any content to the notion of 'society' and its central weakness in its theoretical fixation on nineteenth-century problems, on property rather than administration. Socialists vacillate, and have always vacillated, between a backward-looking elevation of the pre-industrial *Gemeinschaft*, transmuted in fantasy to an organic but spontaneous and ahistorical community without hierarchy, authority or oppressive ideology, and the elevation of a society organized as a rationally planned workshop on bureaucratic-administrative lines, with the state as the centre and foundation of all values and all activities. This is the contradiction noted but hardly solved by Mao Tse-tung when he says:

> Within the ranks of the people, democracy is correlative with centralism, and freedom with discipline. They are the two opposites of a single entity, contradictory as well as united, and we should not one-sidedly emphasize the one to the denial of the other. Within the ranks of the people, we cannot do without freedom, nor can we do without centralism. This unity of democracy and centralism, of freedom and discipline, constitutes our democratic centralism.

The overwhelmingly bureaucratic-administrative character of the Soviet regime, and its increasingly frank elevation of bureaucratic-administrative values, have starkly dramatized one side of socialism and at the same time lost the Soviet Union the admiration of most radical critics of Western society, who refuse to recognize that the real

---

[23] See, for example, V. F. Kotok and N. P. Farberov, 'The Constitution of the USSR— A Developing Fundamental Law for Society and the State', (1973) *Sovetskoe gosudarstvo i pravo*, no. 6, pp. 3–12, translated in (1974) 15 *Soviet Review*, pp. 3–20. Space does not permit us here to discuss the development of law and legal theory in China, on which see the series of three articles by A. E. S. Tay, 'Law in Communist China—Part I', in (1969) 6 *Sydney Law Review*, pp. 153–72, 'Law in Communist China—Part II', in (1971) 6 *Sydney Law Review*, pp. 335–70 and ' "Smash Permanent Rules" ' (see note 2). The development has its own distincive history, but the tensions and theoretical problems are the same: China, as we can now see clearly, does not represent a *new* way.

evils of the Soviet Union are grounded in politics, not administration. On the other hand, the language of Chinese propaganda (until recently) and of the new 1975 Chinese state constitution had about it a homely simplicity and betrayed a seeming concern with the people, and especially with the problem of popular participation in the work of a mass society, which understandably struck responsive chords among those who fear dehumanization and the loss of control over themselves and their environment in the highly fragmented and specialized society of the west. But the language of the Chinese constitution is also the language of the seventeenth-century puritan divines which led to and made possible the Salem witch trials. Listen to the Reverend Thomas Hooker, a man sincerely beloved by his colleagues and a saint according to his own lights:

> Christ has appointed church-censures as good physic to purge out what is evil. All men are made watchmen over the welfare of their brethren, and by virtue of their consociation and combination have power over each other and a judicial way of process against each other in case of any sinful aberration.[24]

In its complete politicization of all aspects of human life, in its elevation of the party and its ideology over the rest of society, in the pervasiveness and the ruthlessness of its pressures on every human individual in a nation or group of nations of more than 800 million persons, the People's Republic of China comes closer to Orwell's *1984* than either Nazi Germany or the USSR. It is morally superior in its much more sparing use of murder as a weapon of control. But the number of suicides in China both before and after the revolution does help to bring out how intolerable life in a *Gemeinschaft* can be, how inescapable its pressures, how hopeless the outlook for those who seek either to protest or to withdraw. It does matter *what* one participates or is forced to participate *in*. 'One's own shirt', says a Russian proverb, 'is nearest one's back'; we resent and fear our own discomforts and lack imagination for the agony of others, especially, as Hume remarked, if they live in a time or a place or in conditions not at all like our own. We yearn for the *Gemeinschaft* if and to the extent that we have never known it; we thrill to millions of Chinese marching in uniform because they are sufficiently *unlike* us to preclude total identification, and we are puzzled when their new leaders, after renewed purges, tell us that what we admired was actually a sham, and that the procedures elevated by the Gang of Four were precisely what some of us always claimed they were—something even worse than bureaucratic control and regularized state oppression.

---

[24] As cited in Ludwig Lewisohn, *The Story of American Literature* (New York, 1939), p. 9.

The primary lesson to be learnt from the history of socialism and the concrete examination of revolutionary communist societies is that neither the abolition of economically significant private property nor the elevation of socialist-communist ideology renders societies homogeneous, conflictless and self-administering. If law withers away, it does so only to give way to force; if the alleged 'social interest' reigns supreme, it does so only because all other interests have been denied the right to be heard and one particular interest has been elevated above them. This happens in times of crisis and violent change; it does not usher in the utopia promised by those who led the revolution. Human society is and will always remain a complex economy of competing interests, claims and requirements. There may have been and still are good laws and bad laws, responsive legal systems and unresponsive ones, imaginative and statesmanlike lawyers and legislators or narrow, rigid and incompetent ones. But the Western legal tradition contains an accumulated body of wisdom in social matters—expressed in legal ideals, precepts, norms, concepts and techniques—that cannot be and has not been swept away by any society seeking peace, justice and security for its citizens, seeking to nurture and protect the life of the individual in a social setting. The central problem for advanced industrial societies in the twentieth century is no longer the problem of private property; it is that of administration and social control, in communist and socialist countries as in the mixed economies of the West. The Austrian Marxist legal philosopher Karl Renner saw this at the very beginning of this century, when he wrote:

Norm and substratum have become so dissimilar, so incommensurable, that the working of property, the way in which it functions, is no longer explained and made intelligible by the property norm; today we must look to the complementary institutions of property. The lives of most of the people, even of the capitalists, are regulated by the law relating to landlord and tenant, their food is controlled by the law of the market, and their clothing, expenditure and pleasures are controlled by the law of wages. Property remains only in the background as a general legal presupposition for the special law that comes into operation, an institution of which we are dimly aware as the necessary consequence of the regrettable fact that there must be someone who is in the last resort responsible for the disposal of any object . . .

A two-fold development is taking place: first, . . . the complementary institutions of private law have deprived the owners of their technical disposal over their property; and secondly,. . . . the common will has subjected property to its direct control, at least from the point of view of the law. Elements of a new order have been developed within the framework of an old society. So it may not be necessary to clamour for prophets whose predictions of the future will flow from esoteric qualities of the soul. It may well be that there is no need to proclaim premiums for those who would draft the new legal constitution of a reasonable social order; perhaps the truth is that we can simply deduce the law of the future from the data supplied by our experience of today and yesterday.[25].

The belief, among socialists and others, that we are heading for a reasonable social order may be less luminous now than it was in Renner; the confidence that we can predict with accuracy the future on the basis of the present may be substantially weaker. But Renner was right in seeing the managerial aspects of ownership and control implied in the direction of labour and the regulatory pretensions of the state as moving to the forefront of modern society and law as therefore remaining at its centre. To think about the implications of that is much more difficult but infinitely more important than demonstrating the class bias of individual judges or shaping the whole of one's conception of society around the needs of homosexuals, deserted mothers and what Marxists used to call the *Lumpenproletariat* and the *demi-monde*.

[25] Karl Renner, *The Institutions of Private Law and Their Social Functions*, as translated by Agnes Schwarzschild in the English edition introduced and annotated by O. Kahn-Freund (London, 1949), pp. 290, 298. Renner already noted the growing divorce between ownership and control, the extent to which property had come to imply the direction of labour and the consequent bureaucratization of capitalism, matched by the growth of state direction and interference.

4
The new criminology

Robert Brown

There is a set of views which, despite the considerable age of some of its members, has been called by its advocates 'the new criminology'. Although these views have a common origin, they remain rather loosely connected, for they are held together, in part, by the more general political sympathies and policy commitments of the criminologists who advance them. In his chapter on 'The New Penology', Professor Hawkins makes it clear what these broader sympathies are, and it would be difficult to improve on the accuracy of his description. What can be done, instead, is to assess the intellectual soundness of several of the criminological views themselves, in particular their soundness as criticism, and thus to answer the somewhat sceptical question, is this yet another transformation without visible change?

The attack on traditional criminology

One basic complaint about which the new critics are in general agreement is that the criminologist's search for characteristic differences between the class of criminals and the class of non-criminals rests upon a false assumption. There are simply no such differences. J. G. Poveda makes this point when he writes: 'This false dichotomy has usually taken expression in the characterization of criminals as belonging to some criminal type. Where earlier criminal type myths attempted to link the criminal to certain physical characteristics or mental deficiencies, the modern myth of the criminal type persists in identifying the criminal with a particular social type—poor, lower class, slum dweller.'[1] On this view, most crimes in Western industrial societies are not committed, as they are commonly said to be, by young, working-class males. To say this is to take a small

[1] 'The Image of the Criminal: A Critique of Crime and Delinquency Theories', *Issues in Criminology* 5 (1970), p. 59.

part of criminal activity for the whole. It is, in Michael Phillipson's words, 'To take crime out of its social context and to try to explain it as the product of a minority of unfortunate individuals apparently "outside" the bounds of conventional society.'[2] Once we make this mistake, so the argument proceeds, it is a natural but further mistake to look for the explanation of such criminal activity in the personal background and social environment of the offenders. Traditional criminologists then raise the question why a particular offender, or a class of offenders, differs from the members of the law-abiding population. What is it in the offender's psychological history or social background, they ask, which has led him to reject, or at least to fail to internalize, those norms which prevent most people from engaging in criminal activity?

But once the problem is envisaged in this way, the critics continue, two consequences are almost inevitable. The first is that the answer to the question why certain individual members of a society behave in a criminal fashion is confused with the answer to a pair of quite different questions, namely (a) why is there ever any criminal behaviour at all in that society? and (b) why do the level and composition of that behaviour fluctuate? According to the new criminologists, it is an obvious error to try to explain the presence of crime generally, or its level and composition in a particular society, by producing explanations of what caused any given member of the society knowingly to violate its criminal laws. The second consequence of looking for the differences between criminals and non-criminals is that the study of criminals comes to be the study of convicted criminals. For how else are we to know where to find our class of genuine criminals? So, in practice, our research on the characteristics of the criminal population will be research only on the population of those people who have been caught and convicted. But since we shall then be investigating the psychological history and social background of only a small sample, we shall have no reasons for believing that it is representative of the much larger unconvicted criminal population. In fact, we have good reason to believe that the sample is not representative. As Phillipson reminds us, 'There have been several studies by sociologists of self-reported crimes which show that the vast majority of individuals, when interviewed anonymously, admit to extensive criminal activity' (p. 83). One American study, for example, 'found that over 90 per cent of their adult sample admitted to the commission of a range of offences for which they could have been gaoled . . . these offences range from . . . many traffic offences or forms of minor larceny, to more serious crimes, including various kinds of violence against the person or more serious forms of theft' (*ibid.*).

[2] *Sociological Aspects of Crime and Delinquency* (London, 1971), p. 245.

Phillipson summarizes these criticisms of much traditional criminology by suggesting that it contains four false assumptions: (1) 'there are universal causes of crime which can be located through criminological research methods which in their turn rely heavily on the use and logic of the statistical methods'; (2) the population can be divided 'into two groups, criminals and non-criminals', and the 'causes of crime can be located by finding factors which significantly differentiate the two groups'; (3) 'if the causes of crime can be located by the study of individual criminals, then the prevention of crime can best be achieved by doing something to these same individuals'; (4) 'although lip service is generally paid to the limitations of official statistics as measures of the "problem", nevertheless they are still typically used as indices of trends in crime' (*ibid.* p. 160).

Of these four assumptions, it is the second, say the critics, which is crucial in the development of traditional errors, for the distinction between criminal and non-criminal types is the direct outcome of a mistaken notion of the problem to be solved. As long as we think that criminal activity is chiefly carried on by a specifiable group in the population, it seems reasonable and important to ask both what causes that group to behave in that way and whether relevantly similar groups elsewhere do the same because universal causes are at work. However, when we learn that criminal activity is widely distributed throughout the general population, these two questions no longer arise. For if there are no features which causally distinguish criminals from non-criminals, it is useless to ask questions which presuppose that there are. Instead, the new criminologists urge, we ought to ask 'why so few people are dealt with by the official mechanisms of social control? If we are all criminal to a degree, do not the key sociological questions concern the processes by which a very small group is selected out and given the official public label of criminal and the effects of such processes? Clearly the social control mechanisms are very highly selective in the legal norms they select for enforcement, in their disposition of organizational resources for control and in whom they actually select out for control' (*ibid*, p. 83). Since convicted criminals form only a small proportion of the violators of criminal laws, it is not merely upon the violators or non-violators that we have to concentrate our attention, but upon the ways in which, and the groups by whom, those criminal laws are created, sustained, enforced and violated. We have to widen our field of view in order to account both for individual participation in criminal activity and, more urgently, for 'the derivation of the "criminal" label (whose content, function and applicability . . . will vary across time, across cultures, and internally with a social structure)'.[3]

[3] Ian Taylor, Paul Walton and Jock Young, *The New Criminology* (London, 1973), p. 224.

Now to these remarks it is necessary to add a word about the ambiguous use here of the phrase 'derivation of the "criminal" label'. The phrase is being used, apparently, to refer to any one or more of three separate problems—firstly, the problem of why a particular sort of behaviour has been made a criminal offence in a specific society; secondly, the problem of why a particular sort of person is prone to be arrested and tried for a particular sort of criminal offence; and thirdly, the problem of what the psychological and social consequences are for people who come to be officially labelled as criminal offenders. The reason why these three problems are all referred to under the same heading by the new criminologists is clear enough. They believe that the sorts of behaviour which are made subject to the penalty of the criminal law in Western industrial societies are those that threaten the property rights and privileges of the power-holding groups. Crime of this type is a primitive form of class warfare by working people against their economic superiors, and the latter try to hold the former in check by means of the criminal law. The police and judiciary are conditioned to penalize severely offences which arise from the precarious and unjust conditions of working-class life; but these same officials treat middle-class offences with the utmost sympathy. Working-class offenders are treated as serious threats to the social order whereas middle-class criminals are treated as being simply mischievous. Thus it is no mystery, the indictment concludes, why criminals come to be thought of as predominantly young, working-class males. Everything in the society conspires to cast them in the role of dangerously criminal youth, and once selected and convicted, the young male offenders will be taught by hard experience to label themselves as permanently criminal.

The general conclusion drawn by the new criminologists is that their predecessors asked the wrong questions as a result of making false assumptions. So the first part of the criminologist's task, these critics would say, is to correct the assumptions and change the questions. Only when he has done this can he hope to make useful recommendations in matters of policy, for it is only then that he will understand the causal factors at work sufficiently well to be able to change them. It is because the traditional criminologist took his problem to be that of explaining the behaviour of individual offenders that he overlooked a much more important problem—that of discovering the general social causes of changes in crime rates. Our ability to alter those rates will depend on our recognition of those causes. Needless to say, some new criminologists believe that the causes have already been discovered. They are the well known inequalities, between social classes, of private wealth, private property, social power, and life-chances.

At this point it is useful to enter an objection so familiar that it would be not worth making if the claims under discussion had avoided an obvious but important error. The objection is that our ability to alter crime rates need not require us to recognize their causes. Just as medical practitioners can produce curative effects with drugs whose biochemical operation is still unknown, so may social engineers recommend measures whose efficiency does not depend upon their being currently explicable. The deliberate control of crime rates is no exception. If, for example, it had been observed that the rates of crimes against property always declined during an economic depression, we might be able to lower them at will by producing a depression; but the success of the operation would not require that we be able to explain why it worked. The point is important here because the political sympathies of many new criminologists lead them to advocate that we adopt their questions because only the answers to them will enable us to intervene effectively in the appropriate social processes. This claim is simply false. However, someone might reply that the new criminologists think it important for the convicted themselves to take political action on their own behalf. To do this efficiently they must understand the character of their plight—and that understanding requires them to possess an explanation of the factors which produce their plight. But, of course, this reply simply repeats the original error that corrective action necessarily requires recognition of causes.

Conversely, our ability to provide a satisfactory explanation of changes in crime rates—or a satisfactory explanation of anything else, for that matter—does not ensure that we have the capacity for effective intervention. So it cannot be argued that the solution of the new questions put forward will lead to the desired social change. All that their solution can ensure is that *if* we can make such a change we shall be able to make it on the basis of knowledge rather than guess work. The importance of the questions and answers proposed by the new criminology will have to be judged on their scientific merit alone; the political uses which they may or may not possess will have to be shown separately.

Is there a criminal type?

Let us now consider the new criminologists' basic complaint against the old—that there are no characteristic differences between the class of criminals and the class of non-criminals, and that the former cannot be identified with a particular social type because criminal behaviour is found plentifully among all social types. The appeal of this claim depends largely on accepting the view that distinguishing between two such classes is the same as attributing different types of crime to different social groups. For one of the points best established by traditional criminology in Western countries is that different types of criminal violations attract different types of violators, violators who are provoked to action in specifiable kinds of circumstances. Thus D. C. Gibbons writes of the United States that: 'bank robberies. . . are usually the work of desperate men. . . carried out as a last resort to solve some. . . crisis in the life of the robber, rather than the acts of criminal gangs';[4] and that 'acts of murder appear to be most frequent among those who have grown up in a "subculture of violence", who have been subjected to a number of disorganizing social influences over an extended period of time, and who are disposed to look on others as potential assailants' (*ibid.* p. 274). But murder is also the outcome of 'situations of marital discord or tavern fights, in which a number of provocative moves and counter-moves of. . . partners culminate' (*ibid.*). Of forcible rape Gibbons says that it is usually committed during a sexually provocative period by 'working-class males from a social situation where exploitative and aggressive themes regarding females are common' (p. 275).

The US report by the President's Commission on Law Enforcement and Administration of Justice summarized the situation thus:

> One of the most fully documented facts about crime is that the common serious crimes that worry people most—murder, forcible rape, robbery, aggravated assault, and burglary—happen most often in the slums of large cities. Study after study in city after city in all regions of the country have traced the variations in rates for these crimes. The results, with monotonous regularity, show that the offences, the victims, and the offenders are found most frequently in the poorest, and most deteriorated and socially disorganized areas of cities.
>
> Studies of the distribution of crime rates in cities and of the conditions of life most commonly associated with high crime rates have been conducted for well over a century in Europe and for many years in the United States. The findings have been remarkably consistent. Burglary, robbery and serious assaults occur in areas characterized by low income, physical deterioration, dependency, racial and ethnic concentrations, broken homes, working mothers, low levels of education and vocational skill, high unemployment, high proportions of single males, overcrowded and substandard housing, high rates of tuberculosis and infant mortality, low rates of home ownership or single family dwellings, mixed land use, and high population density.[5]

All these facts are as well known to the new criminologists as to the old. Why, then, do the former think that 'identifying the criminal with a particular social type' is a 'modern myth'? There seem to be only two feasible explanations. The first is that they believe that all or most of our official statistics on crime are inaccurate because they come from tainted sources, and that the number of criminal offences is neither known nor knowable. Now, that large portions of the figures are very

---

[4] 'Observations on the Study of Crime Causation', *American Journal of Sociology* 77 (1971), p. 273.

[5] *The Challenge of Crime in a Free Society* (Washington, D.C., 1967), p. 35.

poor is not in doubt. But one reason why we know this is because we have additional information provided by some apparently reliable surveys, including self-report studies. If this were not the case, the new criminologists would have much less on which to base their claim. What they have to believe, therefore, is that all and only those figures which tell against their views are suspect. Yet which figures can these be? The same survey of 10,000 American households that showed 'the actual amount of crime in the United States' to be several times greater than the amount revealed by the FBI's United Crime Reports also showed the following: 'The risk of victimization is highest among the lower income groups for all Index offences except homicide, larceny, and vehicle theft; it weighs most heavily on the non-whites for all Index offences except larceny; it is borne by men more often than women, except, of course, for forcible rape; and the risk is greatest for the age category 20 to 29, except for larceny against women, and burglary, larceny, and vehicle theft against men' (*ibid.* p. 39). If we wish to rely, as the new criminologists do, on figures for unreported crimes in general, how can we then reject the associated figures concerning high victimization rates among poor, non-white males? One instance of how high they are for non-white males as compared to white males is provided by the 1971 rates per 100,000 of deaths by homicide—4,927 for non-white males, 500 for white males. The victimization survey of 1966 by the National Opinion Research Center found that for the income group under $6,000 annually the rate of serious crimes against persons was (per 100,000) 748 for blacks and 402 for whites; for the income group of $6,000 or more annually, crimes against property were at the rate (per 100,000) for blacks 3,024 and for whites 1,765. These are substantial differences in victimization. And since we know from the same survey that serious American crimes of these sorts are largely intra-racial—about 80 per cent of black victims had black assailants, and 88 per cent of white victims had white assailants—these victimization rates by race, income and sex mark out not only social types of victims, but also give some indication of the social types of the offenders, since at least half the offences took place in or near the victims' homes.[6]

Of course, while we may be willing to accept these self-reported figures for victimization, we are entitled to be much more suspicious of any conclusions to be drawn from arrest rates. Nevertheless, it is striking that in the United States in 1965 persons 15 to 25 years of age—about 13 per cent of the total population—made up about 80 per cent of arrests for burglaries, 76 per cent of larcenies, 88 per cent of car thefts, 69 per cent of robberies, 64 per cent of forcible rapes, 79 per

[6] P. H. Ehmis, *Criminal Victimisation in the United States: A Report of a National Survey,* The President's Commission on Law Enforcement and Administration of Justice (Washington, D.C., 1967), pp. 30–40.

cent of arrests for arson, and 43 per cent of arrests for negligent manslaughter. The 1965 American arrest rate for vehicle theft, burglary, and larceny varied from 2,467 per 100,000 persons 15 to 17 years old to 55 per 100,000 for persons 50 years old and over. Equally large differences are shown by other American arrest rates: for crimes of violence in 1965, ages 18 to 20 had a rate per 100,000 of 300 while age 50 and over had a rate of 24; for all Index offences plus petty larceny the male rate per 100,000 population was 1,097 and the female 164. It is equally striking, but perhaps more easily accounted for in part, that in 1965 black arrests made up 58 per cent of those for murder, 51 per cent for forcible rape, 58 per cent for robbery, 53 per cent for aggravated assault, and 34 per cent for burglary. Blacks then formed about 10 per cent of the American population. These arrests are sometimes explained as due (a) to prejudice by the police, to the biases introduced by their procedures and to social control by the powerful, and (b) to imposed norms directed at the frustrated, and hence hostile, poor. But we must choose between these two accounts: the first assumes that the arrest rates do not accurately reflect the total volume of offences in a society; the second account tries to explain why the poor contribute disproportionately to this volume. In any case, few criminologist have claimed that well educated, well to do, adult white Anglo-Saxon males make a substantial contribution to the rates for serious assault, theft, burglary, robbery, arson, and forcible rape. If this group commonly practised these crimes would its members remain immune to *scrutiny*, *complaints*, and *arrest*? Whether they would then be dealt with as severely as members of other groups is a different question.

However, Australian data show many similarities to the American data in age and sex distribution. In 1972–3, for example, 17- to 20-year old males made up about 8½ per cent of the total male population of the state of Victoria. But they were charged with a third of the serious assaults, more than half of the robberies, 40 per cent of the rapes, and nearly half of the cases of breaking and entering. For the same period in Tasmania, males between 15 and 26 years of age numbered 40,000 of a total male population of 196,000. They were charged with almost half of the total homicides, half of the rapes, two thirds of the robberies, and 40 per cent of the cases of breaking and entering. In both states the female contribution to these offences was insignificant.

The question, then, is whether age, sex, and racial differences of this order can be disregarded as being merely the result of the collection technique, or whether they are the result of genuine social differences—and if so, what proportion of the former differences can be explained in terms of the latter. What we know of victimization rates by race, sex, and age strongly suggests that they are produced by particular social groups for particular sorts of offences. Whether these social groups amount, in given cases, to social *classes* is a separate and important question. At present there is no reliable answer, one way or the other, to the question, 'What is the *class* distribution of ordinary offences against persons and property—in any particular jurisdiction?'[7] What we do have is information on certain social groups; and some of these undoubtedly belong to different social classes. But to attribute certain kinds and levels of offences to particular groups is not the same as to attribute these offences to the social classes, if any, from which the groups are drawn.

However, there is another way, it might be replied, in which our crime rates are unreliable. This second explanation of why a single criminal social type does not exist is that our statistics do not measure the vast amounts of middle-class occupational (or white-collar) crime. Bribery, corruption, misappropriation, collusion, misrepresentation, price fixing, black marketeering, and many other business crimes go unrepresented in our crime rates because these offences go largely unnoticed, unprosecuted, and unpunished in the criminal courts. If the public took these crimes into account, then criminologists would find it less easy to characterize criminals as being drawn, for the most part, from the most disadvantaged social and economic groups. Why should we not admit what everyone knows—that each social class and ethnic group has its own characteristic forms of criminal behaviour, forms which depend both on the opportunities available and the skills required? But if we did so, the reply might continue, we should find that there were no characteristic and important differences between criminals and non-criminals taken generally, only differences between the kinds of criminal violations displayed by various social and economic strata. Those differences are real enough. For there are many types of criminals, and they belong to many social types rather than to only one.

Thus the point being made by the critics of traditional criminology is twofold—firstly, that ordinary crimes of violence and theft are well distributed throughout the population; and secondly, that in considering the problems of criminal behaviour we must include all those occupational crimes which are grossly under-represented in the work of the criminal courts. Why should these courts concentrate their efforts on the criminal opportunities open to the poor and uneducated while the crimes open only to less poor and better educated are either ignored or dealt with by regulatory agencies?

When the new critic's complaint is put in this familiar way, its force is obvious. But the precise character of that force needs to be made clearer. Thus it is true that studies of self-reported crimes have shown that the overwhelming majority of people, when asked, will admit to

[7] See S. Bosa and J. Ford, 'Social Class and Criminal Behaviour', *The Sociological Review* 19 (1971), pp. 31–52.

having committed criminal offences of which many are serious. However, such studies also show that 'most people do not persist in committing offences' (ibid. p. 44), and that of male juveniles who do, the frequent and serious offenders were predominantly of low social status, poor educational performance, low work skills, and unsatisfactory family relationships.[8] So while it is true that ordinary crimes and violence are well distributed throughout all social and economic classes, it is probably not true that persistent and serious crimes are so distributed: career delinquents, for example, have been found only among low status boys (Hood and Sparks, p. 58). This is one reason why the disadvantaged are so heavily represented among convicted offenders (ibid. pp. 61–3). Moreover, these convicted offenders, at least in the United States, contribute a disproportionate share of the crimes brought to court. The President's Commission found that 'roughly a third of the offenders released from prison will be reimprisoned, usually for committing new offences, within a five year period' (Challenge of Crime, p. 45).

Hence social groups of persistent offenders against the ordinary criminal laws concerning property and person have largely fallen, and still do, into a single social type in Western industrial countries—for studies made in Scandinavia, Britain, Germany, and elsewhere reveal the same pattern as in the United States.[9] The type is precisely that whose existence is denied by the new criminologists: it is that of the poor, the uneducated, and the socially disadvantaged. These features mark quite general differences between persistent and serious violators of the ordinary criminal law and non-persistent and less serious violators of it. These differences are both characteristic and important. They are important because, in many countries, the crimes committed by the disadvantaged—poor people's crimes—have as their chief victims other poor people in the neighbourhood. The new criminologists are indulging in a curious reversal of their egalitarian sympathies if they criticize the criminal courts for trying to protect the disadvantaged from their predators. That the latter are also disadvantaged, or that there are also middle- and upper-class predators of the poor, is hardly a good reason for neglecting the major source of ordinary criminal offences. True, the disadvantaged groups suffer other disabilities than the exposure of their persons and property to attack from their own members. But several surveys have

[8] See the summary in R. Hood and R. Sparks, Key Issues in Criminology (New York, 1970), pp. 54–60. See also M. Gold, 'Undetected Delinquent Behavior', Journal of Research in Crime & Delinquency 13 (1966), pp. 27–46; B. J. Knight and D. J. West, 'Temporary and Continuing Delinquency', British Journal of Criminology 15 (1975), pp. 43–50.

[9] See, for example, J. J. Tobias, Crime and Industrial Society in the Nineteenth Century (London, 1967); H. Mannheim, Comparative Criminology (London, 1965), II, pp. 459–62; Hood and Sparks, pp. 54–61.

shown that direct attack on people's personal safety and property usually worries them more than does occupational crime. Thus in a survey of 600 Sydney households in 1973 the respondents, choosing from the eleven common offences listed, chose as the most serious the four which required physical violence: fifth place was occupied by larceny of valuable goods.[10] Similarly, the Australian Crime-Severity Survey of 1970[11] found that the approximately 1,000 respondents allotted punishment rank as follows, in order of decreasing severity—(1) murder in armed robbery; (2) heroin-selling; (3) armed bank robbery; (4) pack rape; (5) murder of adulterous wife. The misappropriation of large amounts of company funds ranked seventh after rape, but the penalty suggested for misappropriation (imprisonment for six months to two years) was much lighter than that given for rape (imprisonment for three to five years). These results are similar to those obtained in San Francisco by D. C. Gibbons: in descending order of severity were murder, robbery, manslaughter, burglary, rape, embezzlement, and anti-trust violations. The two white collar crimes of misrepresentation in advertising and tax evasion were much further down the list. This response is quite rational for, as Daniel Bell put it, 'from the viewpoint of a person who has been held up or whose house has been burglarized, the result is a direct and immediate loss, whereas the defalcations and frauds of business are spread, like a tax, on the community at large. When an individual speaks of crime, he is thinking of something which affects him directly.' [12]

Business crime vs. personal crime

Now when a new criminologist speaks of crime he is seldom thinking of anything which affects him as directly as a blow on the head. He is thinking of the immense financial costs to the community of white-collar crime, of occupational offences generally, of organized vice, and of business racketeering. However, it is by no means clear that these high costs of doing business or of gaining illegal pleasure can be substantially lowered by increased use of the criminal courts rather than by the use of other means. It may well be true, as some studies suggest, that in terms of reconviction rates 'fines and discharges are much more effective than either probation or imprisonment for first offenders and recidivists of all age groups' (Hood and Sparks, pp. 188–9). Regulatory agencies often have the power to order the payment of fines which are enforceable in law. They can make such

[10] A. A. Congalton and M. Najman, 'Unreported Crime', Statistical Report, 12, New South Wales Bureau of Crime, Statistics and Research, n.d.

[11] P. R. Wilson and J. W. Brown, *Crime and the Community* (St. Lucia, Queensland, 1973), pp. 52–4.

[12] In *The End of Ideology* (New York, 1960), p. 417.

orders as well as can the criminal courts. Such agencies also have, or could have, various disciplinary powers: these include warnings and orders to desist, suspension, and then deregistration, of practitioners or organizations. At the very least, these agencies can force disclosure of crucial information that is illegally withheld. So, unless we have some reason to believe that imprisonment will be more effective in deterring and reforming occupational criminals than it is in the case of other criminals, we have no occasion to extend its use. In particular, the new criminologists—who wish to transform social institutions instead of merely correcting the offender—have no reason for enlarging what they take to be an evil and useless practice.

Again, it is clearly much more expensive and complex to bring prosecution against either criminal activity organized as a business, or business activity that becomes illegal practice, than it is to prosecute the offences of individual criminals. Both racketeering and white-collar crime can take place on a gigantic scale, a scale which requires that special bodies of technically trained people devote their full time to investigating and prosecuting them. The American Securities Exchange Commission, for example, used eight lawyers for twenty months merely to investigate the transactions between the Vesco group and the IOS mutual funds. Because IOS was an offshore manager of mutual funds and investment trusts, and thus not subject to much legal regulation and scrutiny, the Vesco group was able, it is alleged, to remove illegally some $500 million US dollars worth of IOS funds. 'Concerted action by the inter-agency committee resulted in three fifths of the plundered assets being blocked. By all accounts that left the Vesco group with between $200 and $300 million secreted in offshore havens, in foreign banks, hidden trusts, and little known Hong Kong trading companies.'[13]

The scale of operations conducted by criminal cartels is similarly large. The President's Commission of 1967 reported that even then the city of Los Angeles had a 55-man unit simply to gather information about the operations of organized criminals (*Challenge of Crime*, p. 197) in such activities as gambling, narcotics, loan-sharking, the raiding of labour union funds, and the obtaining of corrupt concessions of all kinds. When to these activities are added the size of the losses from the commission of white-collar crimes like price fixing, defective construction, misappropriation of funds, and the violations of safety, health, and licensing statutes, the magnitude of the problem of business and quasi-business crime is obvious enough. But how would treating it as just another form of criminal activity—on a par with burglary and homicide—help to control it? The new crimin-ologists have produced no evidence to show that bringing all

[13] Alexander Cockburn, 'Million Dollar Yeggs', *The New York Review of Books*, 20 (March 1975), p. 21, reviewing and quoting from *Vesco* by R. A. Hutchison.

these offences within the jurisdiction of the criminal courts would serve any useful purpose. After all, many of the offences are already dealt with by those courts. How could increasing their work load improve their performance?

Now, to this question it may be replied that the basic point at issue is not whether the criminal courts will try such cases of occupational crime. Rather it is whether the educated population is willing to have social institutions that treat business crime at least as firmly and severely as they do working-class crime. But the difficulty with this question is in knowing how to interpret it. On one interpretation, it amounts only to urging us to use the same forms and severity of punishment for both sorts of offenders, a suggestion that would be more acceptable if it were not harnessed to the criticism that traditional forms of punishment have failed. Applying admittedly bad procedure in fair shares to all offenders is vindictiveness—an immoral response of the kind which the new penologists accuse their predecessors of supporting. On another interpretation, the proposal is simply to treat business or quasi-business crime as a greater social evil than any other sort of crime. But insofar as this proposal is a recommendation for changes in our policy preferences, it is not clear that the proposal ought to be accepted. There is little doubt that in some countries the economic loss from business crime far exceeds that from all other forms of crime. It is also certain that much physical harm to people results from business malpractice: poisonous foods, injurious drugs, unsafe machines, defective buildings and goods are the most familiar examples. And it is plausible to go on to argue, at least in the absence of much empirical investigation, that malpractice in such volume permanently worsens the functioning of the social institutions on which it is parasitic. Nevertheless, there is an obvious and important difference between a situation in which a person must constantly stand armed guard over his person and his property—or employ trained dogs and ingenious devices to do so—and one in which his greatest danger comes from not being on constant watch for malpractice and swindles which affect him personally. The difference is simply that successful malpractice and swindles require the existence of a milieu in which many honest negotiations take place, whereas successful violence, burglary, and theft do not require the existence of a previously secure and peaceful environment. Before commercial crime can flourish there must be enough ordinary commercial traffic to make piracy possible and worthwhile. But before violence and offences against personal property can dominate human relationships, there need be no analogous flow of amicable intercourse. The relationships may begin in rape, robbery, assault and burglary, and remain forever after in that state.

Thus the parasitic crimes of commerce and industry presuppose the existence of their well developed hosts. The crimes of personal violence and the offences against personal property do not presuppose the existence of any such highly developed institutions. These crimes can, and do, take place in any society, however simple. To the extent that they flourish, the basic services provided by the social group are endangered. A community which cannot control the physical aggression—the homicide, assault, rape and robbery—of its members, and their offences against each other's personal property, will not have to worry about controlling their more complex antisocial behaviour, for the community will never reach the stage at which the problem arises. The harm which results from business crime is, in this sense, less basic than that which results from direct attack on person and property. Because it is less basic to him, business crime is taken to be less serious by the individual victim, and it is this difference which is marked by our present Western systems of differential punishment. To advocate changing this, so as to turn business crime and individual attack on a person and his property into offences of at least equal seriousness, is to advocate that each person should express no more concern for major threats to his personal safety and property than for threats which are often, though not always, minor ones for him individually, but which collectively are of major importance. In addition, it is to suggest, given our perennially limited resources, that either some of the resources now devoted to the control of these personal threats be redirected to meet these communal threats or that additional resources be applied to the latter rather than the former. Our preference schedule ought, then, to give the remedies of the two sorts of offence something like equal rank, or perhaps reverse the present order.

But is this a reasonable policy? Ought we to contemplate with more satisfaction the existence of a society in which violence to people and their personal property is customary than of one in which racketeering, business and white-collar crime are common? And if the majority of working-class people had to choose, as by hypothesis they do, between these alternatives, is it clear that they would, and should, prefer to be victims of constant violent offences against their persons and property instead of victims of pervasive fraud? To both questions the answer is obviously 'no' for the reason already suggested—namely that a fraud-ridden society must retain social relationships which swindlers can caricature, whereas a violence-ridden group need retain nothing but attackers and victims. If we are forced to choose, in the extreme case, between coping with offences which make social life impossible and coping with offences that simply make it malevolent, then obviously we must choose the latter and try to improve in future. It is only the fact that we never actually have to make this choice that allows some criminologists to claim, with any sort of plausibility, that business and quasi-business crime is a greater social evil than any other type of crime. What they can reasonably claim is something rather different: that given a certain level and variety of ordinary crime, then additional resources directed against business crime will alleviate more misery and cost than they will if directed toward reducing still further the rates for such offences as homicide and robbery. Thus the benefits to be achieved by this procedure are at the margin; they presuppose that ordinary crimes are occurring at tolerable rates and that the resources needed for their control are not put in serious jeopardy by other uses. Yet is this all that is being urged by people who wish us to treat business crime at least as severely and firmly as we treat ordinary crime? If so, they are urging a cause that has no opponents. If this is not the question at issue, which question is?

Changing the criminologists' questions

Let us now return to the other issues raised by the new criminologists. They suggest that the myth of a criminal type encourages the misguided attempt to explain all criminal behaviour in terms of the social and psychological background of individual agents, a background which causally distinguishes them from non-criminal agents. The attempt has then led traditional criminologists, the critics say, to ignore the difference between this problem and two other more important problems: (a) Why is there ever any crime at all in that society? (b) Why does the level and composition of its criminal behaviour fluctuate when it does—or why does it remain steady? The answer to all three questions has been sought by investigating the background of convicted offenders, and it is the details of that background which have been expected to yield the answer to each of the three questions. The investigation has been misguided, the critics continue, because each of the questions requires a different answer. Only the belief in the existence of a criminal type has led people to think that much the same answer would serve for all three questions. For if all, or most, criminal behaviour in a given society is produced by members of a distinctive and identifiable group, then the details of their social and psychological histories may well explain their individual actions and, in addition, explain why there is any crime at all among them. These same details, insofar as they explain the individual's frequency of offence, may also explain the general rate. Such a simple and general account of both the existence of crime and of fluctuations in its rate is not logically or empirically outrageous, and studies of the background of convicted offenders can be, and have been, used in support of this kind of explanation. But the new criminologists remind us that when our belief in the existence of a criminal type or class is abandoned, then any explanation which relies on its existence must also be given up.

However, as we saw earlier, the criminal disadvantaged probably do form a genuine type: its existence is not a myth. Yet the fact that in certain societies there is actually such a type does not compel us to give much the same answer to all three questions. If the criminally disadvantaged merely contribute to the general crime rate, then instancing their presence cannot be used to explain why the society has any crime at all. And even if the disadvantaged were to produce all the criminal behaviour in a society at any given period, our three questions could still have three different answers. The common factors which explained all the individual acts of delinquency at a given period might not explain the presence of any delinquent acts of another period since the causal influences on the disadvantaged might change. In that case there might be a different answer to each of the three questions: why did this person commit that offence then? why is there ever any ordinary crime at all in this society? and why does the society have this crime rate at time t?. Hence, whatever encouragement the investigation of the criminal disadvantaged has given to mixing together these questions, there is not, and never was, any good reason why such an investigation should do so.

In the event, what the new criminologists have called 'a confusion of questions in traditional criminology' is more accurately called 'a desire for a change of questions by the new criminologists'. Practitioners of the latter think that they can give a general and correct answer in terms of socioeconomic inequalities to the question, why is there ever any ordinary crime at all in Western industrial societies? Because they believe that they can, they also believe that the remaining two questions are comparatively unimportant, for these two questions, as traditionally interpreted, presuppose a mistaken search for the factors arising from the peculiarities of the agent's history rather than from the causal influences exerted by his socioeconomic position. And it is the latter which chiefly determines whether he acts illegally. Thus Daniel Bell, writing of the high rates of criminal offences by young male blacks in the United States, said:

> Crime of this sort represents a form of 'unorganized class struggle' . . . . These are lower-class crimes, and the negro makes up the bulk of the lower class . . . At the turn of the century, the majority of such crimes were committed predominantly by the Irish, later by the Italians, then by the Slavs. Today it is the negro and to a lesser extent the Puerto Rican who, in a marginal position, play this role (p. 157).

It is the occupancy of the same social role, then, which chiefly accounts for the illegal behaviour, not the many differences in personality and social background of the occupants.

There are two obvious points to be made to this general view. One is that very few criminologists of the past have thought that the socioeconomic position of their lower-class subjects was not causally important. The question which concerned these investigators, however, was why, *given* general poverty and deprivation, some of the disadvantaged turned to criminal activity and some did not. This perfectly sensible question has to be answered as much by new criminologists as it was by those of the past. It has to be answered because otherwise the existence of a lower class does not explain the presence of ordinary crime. It is no answer to say that poverty and inequality produce it, for the question at issue is to what extent, if any, this is so and what other conditions are required. Thus both El Salvador and Spain are poor countries, with great inequalities of income. Yet the former had, in 1971, for male deaths by homicide a rate of 4,916 per 100,000; the latter had a rate of 21. These two rates are the highest and lowest, respectively, of the 46 countries which were thought by the United Nations Statistical Office to register at least 90 per cent of all deaths. Greece, another poor country, had a rate of 48, the Netherlands, a wealthy country, a rate of 46. Within the social democracies of the Scandinavian bloc, the rates varied from 53 in Denmark to 282 in Finland. And within the 'socialist' countries of Eastern Europe, the rate for Bulgaria (295) was much higher than that for Czechoslovakia (123).

Hence, investigating the personality and social differences between two sorts of disadvantaged groups is the only, and therefore the best, way we have of discovering the criminalizing effects of deprivation upon people actually exposed to it. The answer to this problem is logically presupposed by the claim about the causal importance of lower-class status. Therefore it is a mistake to believe, as some new criminologists do, either that the question answered by the claim is a substitute for, or causally more important than, the other, more limited, question.

There is a second reply to be made here. It is that the question, why is there ever any ordinary crime at all in Western industrial societies? is ill framed. Does it mean (a) why are there ever offences against persons and property in any society? or (b) why are there more (or less) such offences in Western industrial societies than in some others? Both versions are troublesome. The first invites the empty answer: because there is always a very large number of reasons why people do not, or cannot, conform to the criminal laws of their particular society; people become, for example, angry, impatient, forgetful, greedy, fearful, and so do not always observe legal regulations. What other, more useful, answer can we give? One attempt goes like this: 'under certain conditions a resolution in social arrangements could precipitate moral and social consensus . . . . Only when authority is both substantively and formally under control of its subjects . . . can one assume the persistence (in the sense implied by Dahrendorf) of some kind of "permanent readjustment" ' (Taylor, Walton and Young, pp. 251–2).

Yet no matter what sort of authority relationship this might be, the resulting consensus might reduce, but would not eliminate, criminal offences against persons. One man can injure another in anger even though both agree, in calmer moments, that their differences should be solved by negotiation. At best, social consensus might eliminate the criminal consequences of the class struggle—in particular, certain offences against property such as burglary, robbery, and theft; but that would still leave a great number of offences untouched, and especially those in unstratified societies where differences in property ownership are not great.

Of course the question need not receive an empty answer. If we take the question to be, what social forces constrain people from violating laws and social rules? we are raising the most basic question in criminology. But then the answer to it applies to all human societies and has nothing special to do with the inequalities of Western industrial societies: their types and rates of rule breaking will simply illustrate this more general answer.

Version (b) of the question raises a problem of more interest to us here. It may or may not be true that some Western industrial societies have higher rates of comparable crimes than some non-Western and non-industrial societies. Clearly, the question would have to be investigated and the comparisons, as we shall see, would be difficult to draw at best. What is of more importance is how we are to explain those differences which we believe do exist. Consider the implications of the following argument; it is taken from the volume *Law, Order and Power* (Reading, Mass., 1971) by W. J. Chambliss and R. B. Seidman. The authors begin by saying:

> Characteristically, in primitive societies we find a much higher degree of consensus on norms, and a higher degree of internalization of those norms, than is the case in complex societies. That this is true is not surprising, since the range of experiences of the members of the primitive group are more similar than in complex societies, since communication among the members is more intimate, and since changes in the set of life conditions are more gradual and therefore less likely to lead to rapidly changing normative systems (pp. 25–6).

The authors then go on to distinguish two different goals of a tribunal in the settlement of disputes. One is compromise, the other is norm-enforcement.

> Whether the principal objective of dispute-settling is continued relationships or not determines whether the tribunal will base itself on 'give a little, get a little', or 'winner take all'. In the one case, a bargaining relationship is established during the dispute-settling process. The aim of the bargain is not to determine that one side or the other breached the

norm at issue so much as it is to discover a compromise solution which will leave neither party so strongly aggrieved as to make future relationships impossible. If, on the other hand, the tribunal is indifferent whether the parties will live together after the dispute-settlement, then there is no reason why it should not determine unequivocally whether the defendant in fact violated the norm, and then award a decision based on the principle of 'winner taking all' (p. 29).

It is true that bargaining sometimes takes place before tribunals which use the latter principle. But this sort of compromise is aimed at saving time and cost; it is convenience which is aimed at, not the restoration of the previous relationship (*ibid.* pp. 29–30).

Now each of these two goals of dispute-settlement is found in a particular sort of society. At one extreme is the simple subsistence economy with a simple technology, little differentiation of roles and little social stratification. At the opposite extreme is the other sort: it has much differentiation of specialized roles, much interchange of goods and services, a high level of technology, and a high degree of social stratification. Of these two sorts of society, Chambliss and Seidman write:

[In the first sort] every man is dependent in times of crisis on his family and neighbours, a relationship that cannot readily be dissolved if life is to continue. Relatively simple norms of behaviour are learned through elementary socialization, and are enforced through sanctions in which the community at large participates . . . . Formal institutions to sanction the breach of the norms are not required; institutions to maintain social solidarity are.

In a complex society, on the other hand, the opposite it true . . . it is the goods and services which are important, not the identities of the individuals performing those services. The relatively high level of technology reduces the threat of starvation and death, and hence lowers the requirement for mutual support in the future as between any particular individuals. Easy communication at once raises the level of interdependence upon the system as a whole, but reduces the interdependence of specific individuals on each other . . . the institutionalization and enforcement of complex norms and roles in conditions of alienation require more formal processes. In such conditions, whether or not litigants 'live together' after the dispute is unimportant.

As a result of these different characteristics, the dispute-settlement processes of the two kinds of societies will be markedly different. . . . The lower the level of complexity of a society, the more emphasis will be placed in the dispute-settling process upon reconciliation; the more complex the society, the more emphasis will be placed on rule-enforcement (pp. 31–2).

Chambliss and Seidman conclude by saying:

The more economically stratified a society becomes, the more it becomes necessary for the dominant groups in the society to enforce through coercion the norms of conduct which guarantee their supremacy . . . the more the social structure creates and enforces inequality, the more the life experiences of various groups differ and consequently the norms internalized by people in different strata can be expected to vary as well. Under such circumstances, the central thrust of the dispute-settling process shifts from accomplishing an accommodation between the disputants, and thus their reconciliation, to the enforcement of the rule by imposition of a sanction.

The less stratified the society, the more emphasis will be placed in the dispute-settling process on reconciliation; the more stratified the society, the more emphasis will be placed on rule-enforcement.

Where disputes are settled by compromise, it is indifferent to the tribunal what the precise content of the norm is, because this content is not so important as the search for an appropriate middle position between the parties that will re-establish their original relationship. Norms are appealed to in the argument before the tribunal, but the decision of compromise negates the precise ascertainment of the applicable, authoritative norm.

[But] as soon as disputes must be settled on a winner-take-all basis . . . the forum for settling disputes must also determine the correct content of the norm . . . in cases where the norm is unclear, the agency is required to create a new authoritative norm to resolve the problem (pp. 33–5).

Changing the criminologists' answers

Now the bearing of these remarks by Chambliss and Seidman on our problem is obvious. For if societies can be classified in terms of the method by which they settle disputes—on the one hand, by rule-enforcement and, on the other hand, by reconciliation—then not only are two different goals being sought, but two different ways of identifying, and hence counting, offences are being used. In societies with strict rule-enforcement each *violation* will count as an offence, and one task of the investigator will be to determine the scale of unreported violations. But in societies which employ compromise, only *disputes* will be counted, and only a proportion of apparent norm-violations will give rise to these; it is the clash of disputants that matters, not the infraction of a rule. Moreover, since the norms will be vague from the outset, their cash value will be fixed by the accumulation of dispute-settlements. Thus, in the absence of a dispute, there may well be doubt, in specific cases, as to whether a norm has been violated, and indeed, some uncertainty as to the content of the supposed norm. Because mere norm-violations will be of no great concern, the content of these norms will be vague; hence what constitutes their violation will be correspondingly difficult to discover. In this way lack of interest in norm-enforcement produces vagueness of norms, and this in turn produces a difficulty in identifying violations which leads to increasing disinterest in the enforcement of norms.

For our purposes here, the conclusion to be drawn from this difference between the two methods of settling disputes is simple. It is that we cannot sensibly compare crime rates, and all that they represent in the form of social behaviour, between societies which use two such different ways of identifying and dealing with offences. To count norm-infringements—whether or not they be crimes without victims—is one thing; to count only those infringements which have complaining victims is to count something quite different. A comparison of two such sets of figures cannot help to answer the question at issue, namely: why are there more (or less) ordinary criminal offences in Western industrial societies than in some other societies? Now it may be replied, as an objection, that the complainants in a reconciliation system can be officials just as easily as in an enforcement system, and that therefore there need be no arithmetical difference, in principle, between counting disputes with them and counting infringements of the norms which they are charged to uphold. But this reply will not do. It cannot simply offer us an enforcement procedure in the guise of a reconciliation system, and thus amalgamate two different roles. If the officials are external arbiters, then they cannot act as complainants in the cases where they mediate. As complainants they must either act as agents of norm-enforcement—which by definition they are debarred from doing in a reconciliation system—or they must abandon their roles as officials and bargain like anyone else. In doing the latter they may become recognized and principled inciters of dispute, but not officials in the sense required by the objection: they cannot be official agents of compromise in cases which they themselves both bring and arbitrate, and whose outcome they then help to enforce.

Now it is an empirical question, one subject to evidence, whether simple societies commonly use compromise methods whereas complex societies use the procedures of norm-enforcement. But even if no such general division is to be found among actual societies, there is a distinction here which we can use to recharacterize the most basic of the issues raised earlier, namely that of the new criminologists' demand for a change of questions. For we began this discussion by noting that such views are closely connected with the more general political sympathies of the criminologists who advance them. Thus when new criminologists like Taylor, Walton, and Young suggest that 'under certain conditions a revolution in social arrangements could precipitate moral and social consensus' they are giving voice to a widespread yearning for a new reconciliation society, one in which the desire for, and need of, norm-enforcement is at a minimum. They are opposed to the formal institutions which are necessary to detect, hear and penalize cases of infractions, since a system of reconciliation would largely eliminate the necessity for this apparatus of strict norm-enforcement. Under reconciliation there would be no great need to correct deviant agents since the distinction between them and conventional agents would disappear as the subject matter of criminology. Instead, we should be confined to the study of conciliation and arbitration between conflicting, but commonly legitimate, interests.

However, if Chambliss and Seidman are correct, the difficulties of creating such a situation are obvious enough. Firstly, there is a direct causal influence exerted by the combination of role differentiation and social stratification on the procedure of settling disputes, so that any attempt to change the latter will require changes in the former. Secondly, the complex role differentiation and social stratification of modern industrial societies are themselves the causal result, in part, of an advanced technology with its vast interchange of goods and services. We do not yet know how closely connected with each other any of these factors is; so we do not know, in brief, whether it is possible in practice to have a modern industrial society which settles most of its members' disputes chiefly by compromise rather than by norm-enforcement, and by compensation rather than by punishment. Nor do we know whether most *criminal* disputes can be settled by informal mediation rather than by formal arbitration or by norm-enforcement. Can an industrial society, one in which 'the life experiences of various social groups differ greatly', develop new forms of social organization which will make participatory sanctions possible? The new criminologists offer us no information on which to base an answer. Such evidence as we have comes from elsewhere, and we can remind ourselves of it briefly.

Perhaps the correlation most fully established by the older criminologists is that between increasing urbanization and increasing level of ordinary criminal offences. One common way of accounting for this high correlation is in terms of the decreasing influence of primary social bonds: as the size of the neighbouring population increases, so does the number of strangers—people between whom there exist no continuing relationships of mutual aid. If it should turn out that the absence of such relationships helps to account for the increased level of criminal offences in urban conditions, then we must face the question whether reconciliation can be an effective method of settling disputes between strangers. At present, almost all our examples of the successful use of conciliation and arbitration come from disputants who have continuing relationships with each other.

Can reconciliation work without such relationships? The force of this question is made clear in a paper entitled 'Two Forms of Dispute Settlement Among the Kpelle of West Africa' by J. L. Gibbs, Jr. In contrasting Kpelle courtroom hearings with Kpelle moots or 'house palavers', he writes:

> Kpelle courtroom hearings are basically coercive and arbitrary in tone . . . . As a result, the court is limited in the manner in which it can handle some types of disputes. The court is particularly effective in settling cases such as an assault, possession of illegal charms, or theft where the litigants are not linked in a relationship which must continue after the trial. However, most of the cases brought before a Kpelle court are cases involving disputed rights over women, including matrimonial matters which are usually cast in the form of suits for divorce. The court is particularly inept at settling these numerous matrimonial disputes because its harsh tone tends to drive spouses farther apart rather than to reconcile them. The moot, in contrast, is more effective in handling such cases.[14]

Gibbs goes on to discribe the 'house palaver'. It is 'an informal airing of a dispute which takes place before an assembled group which includes kinsmen of the litigants and neighbours from the quarter'. The group usually hears domestic matters—'alleged mistreatment or neglect by a spouse, an attempt to collect money paid to a kinsman for a job which was not completed, or a quarrel among brothers over the inheritance of their father's wives' (p. 370). The moot differs from the courtroom hearing in a number of important respects: the moot discussion occurs soon after the dispute; the moot takes place in familiar and non-intimidating surroundings; the conduct of the proceedings lies with the disputants; relevance is construed widely; the solution is by consensus with 'attribution of fault to both parties'; the mediator's powers are limited to mild penalties; and there is public proffering and acceptance of apology to 'indicate that each party has no further grievances' (p. 373).

For our purposes here two of Gibbs's conclusions are of special interest. The first is that the success of a moot depends upon the cooperation of the litigants: 'Each party must be willing to list his grievances, to admit his guilt, and make an open apology. The moot, like psychotherapy, is impotent without well motivated clients' (p. 377). The second conclusion is that the court and the moot have 'complementary functions'. The moot tries to reconcile the partners in marital disputes whereas the courts usually grant divorces. But we ought not to assume that all marriages should be preserved. Some

---

[14] In D. Black and M. Mileski (eds), *The Social Organization of Law* (New York, 1973), pp. 369–70. Reprinted from 'The Kpelle Moot: A Therapeutic Model for the Informal Settlement of Disputes', *Africa* 33 (1963), pp. 1–10.

marriages produce bad social consequences, and in recognizing this the court decides an issue with which the moot may not be able to deal (p. 378). Let us consider these two conclusions and their relationship a little further.

The cooperation of litigants in moots—or informal settlements of disputes generally—is itself dependent upon the existence of certain sorts of social arrangements. Thus Nader and Metzger contrast two different ways in which marital disputes are dealt with in two Mexican communities and try to account for the difference.

> In both communities, husbands and wives in conflict recognize the authority of senior family males as well as the authority of the community court. However . . . the crucial fact is that family heads assume exclusive rights to judge such conflicts in the Chiapas town and their judgements are non-appealable, while in the Oaxaca community spouses make further attempts to reduce their conflict by appeal to the community court. We suggest that such non-appealable outcomes occur when the tie between the couple in conflict and their senior family males holds great potential for the exchange of scarce goods and resources, and when there exists no substitute relationship which is nearly as productive. A father will be able to maintain his authority over his son only if the latter sees some pay off as a result; indeed, a father will be interested in maintaining strict authority over his son only if it benefits the father himself.[15]

What are the conditions which alter 'social payoffs'? The authors say:

> In the Oaxaca town, limited authority of senior family males is associated with early inheritance, separate residence, readily available substitutes for both spouses and parents with respect to sex and subsistence, and the deliberate refusal of families to accept responsibility for marriages they have not arranged. The court assumes the responsibility lost or abandoned by the family and exercises authority over marriage vested in it as a representative of the state. In the Chiapas community, delayed inheritance, patrisponsored residence, and the absence of spouse or parent-substitutes outside these relationships tend to support the authority of senior male lineals in the resolution of conflict between spouses. The role that the court plays is residual (p. 104).

In a footnote to this the authors add: 'It would seem that in the Oaxaca town marital conflicts are not considered an offence against the extended family, but rather an offence which threatens public or town stability.'

What this case show us, in brief, is that continuing relationships represent a continuing exchange of scarce goods and services; that

[15] L. Nader and Duane Metzger, 'Conflict Resolution in Two Mexican Communities' in Black and Mileski, pp. 101–2. Reprinted from *American Anthropologist* 65 (1963), pp. 584–92.

such exchanges can be created and maintained by certain patterns of authority; and that these patterns, in turn, are supported by such exchanges. Early inheritance, separate residence, alternative sources of nurture and affection—these are social arrangements which *prima facie* act against continuing social relationships and their rewards. Yet these are the arrangements which increasingly characterize industrial societies. Such arrangements lessen the ability of kin and friends to influence certain litigants in the desired ways: marital disputes, for example, can no longer be settled outside the courts. As the power of the family to control rewards for compliance is lessened, the power of the state authority to impose penalties for non-compliance is increased.

The process by which this change takes place is well illustrated in the case of Japan. The traditional preference of the Japanese for extrajudicial settlements is well known. Takeyoshi Kawashima writes, for example: 'A railroad was involved in a total of 145 traffic accidents which caused physical injury during the period from April 1960 to September 1960; but not a single case was handled by attorneys. . . . Of the total of 327 accidents which caused physical injury and involved another railroad in 1960, not a single case was brought to court, and only one case was handled by an attorney.'[16] Kawashima also found that in 1960 there were four companies whose taxis were involved in 235 personal injury cases and 2,567 cases of property damage. Only two of the cases went to litigation (p. 60). He suggests that the explanation for this lies in the fact that litigation disrupts the organization of traditional social groups which favour hierarchical status, flexible roles, agreement by consensus, and group stability. All these features were encouraged by the common Japanese resort to reconciliation and conciliation in the settlement of disputes; decisions leading to the victory of one party over the other were avoided. However, in recent years the changes in the status system and the increasingly legalistic needs of industrial capitalism have helped to weaken the social controls exercised by traditional groups. In consequence, a large number of family disputes previously settled by family councils or by mediators are taken to the family courts in large cities. Now 'it is not at all rare for parties to be aware of their legal rights and to insist upon them so strongly that reconcilement becomes at times quite difficult. Parties to *chōtei* [state mediation committees] cases have frequently complained that lay mediators did not pay sufficient attention to their rights under the law . . . . The transition is irretrievably in process, and the outcome is clear' (*ibid.* pp. 73–4).

But it is important to notice that when disputes arose between,

---

[16] 'Dispute Settlement in Japan' in Black and Mileski, p. 59. Reprinted from 'Dispute Resolution in Contemporary Japan' in *Law in Japan: The Legal Order in a Changing Society*, edited by A. T. von Mehren (Cambridge, Mass., 1963), pp. 41–72.

rather than within, traditional social groups the procedures of settlement were quite different. Mediation often resulted in 'peace treaties'. If it did not, the 'rule of power' prevailed. The weaker party had to resort to a law suit. Thus courtroom disputes between villages over rights of common in land and between lenders and debtors were common in pre-industrial Japan. In fact, debt collectors often used intimidation and violence, even though these were criminal offences (*ibid.* pp. 62–4). This is another example of the general point referred to previously: the success of mediation requires a set of continuing relationships between the disputants. When we destroy those social institutions which promote cooperation by the disputants, we produce a social vacuum which formal legal procedures must fill if disputes are to be settled by peaceful means. The reason that suits for breach of contract among American businessmen are still uncommon is that more 'effective non-legal sanctions' are available. They tend to ensure that offending firms will be penalized in the most direct way, namely by not receiving further business either from their victims or from those who learn of the breaches.[17] The evidence strongly suggests, then, that mediation and arbitration, especially in an industrial society, can succeed only to the extent that the exchange relationship is viewed by the participants as a continuing one which will produce future benefits for both parties. Where the relationship is either transitory or non-productive, or both, disputes will be settled, on the one hand, by hit and run procedures, and on the other hand, by resort to the law. Under the social conditions in which one of these is habitually employed within a population, so will the other be. For the social relationships in an industrial society which make the latter necessary also make the former attractive. And, of course, once either of them is common, it acts to enlarge the other.

Hence, it is true that the desire on the part of new criminologists to replace strict norm-enforcement by conciliation would demand that we produce new primary social groups, ones capable under industrial conditions of controlling the behaviour of their members by informal sanctions. But in doing so we should have to be careful not to make relationships among these primary groups so temporary and non-rewarding that disputes between the groups themselves could be settled only by legal means. The problems which arise in carrying out these two operations are considerable. Modern business and industrial organization owes much of its effectiveness to its reliance, for example, on the predictable legal consequences of the activities of employees: if those habitual consequences are to be negated by 'flexible role-behaviour' and mediation, then long-range planning, both economic and technological, will need to have its procedures revised in

[17] See, for example, S. Macaulay, 'Non-Contractual Relations in Business: A Preliminary Study', *American Sociological Review* 28 (1963), pp. 55–67.

sympathy. But will it be possible to do so? Can the General Motors Corporation be run successfully as a *Gemeinschaft*? is a familiar question. It has yet to be answered.

In any case, there are more narrowly legal questions to be answered. In the new conciliation society, would all disputes become private delicts and tort breaches? Would the nature of the offence depend in some intimate way upon the relationship between the plaintiff and the accused? And if compensation is to be favoured over punishment, would we dispense with the requirement of *mens rea* and the assessment of degrees of guilt? The answer to each of these questions affects the views which we may reasonably hold on likely, and desirable, social changes. For this reason it is worth asking also, how much of the appeal of conciliation for the new criminologist lies in its loose association with compensation. The association is loose because we could, and do, have strict norm-enforcement systems which use compensation instead of punishment; and many reconciliation systems employ mild penalties against both parties. A system of strict norm-enforcement does not always appear in tandem with a policy of severe punishment. The former is compatible with a policy of mild penalties which do not make impossible a continuing relationship between the litigants.

It is useful of the new criminologists to have raised all these persistent problems yet again. However, it would be much more useful if they were now to go on to specify in some detail the social conditions required by, and sufficient for, the urban folk-society of the future. To sketch that particular transformation of law, justice, and morals would take them far beyond the bounds of criminology. But then exceeding their traditional brief is a course on which the new criminologists have already embarked in substituting the study of social deviancy for that of merely criminal behaviour.

5

The new penology

Gordon Hawkins

I The new penology

Those who read *The New Criminology*[1] in the hope that the authors may throw some light on the theoretical and practical problems of punishment will be disappointed. Unlike the majority of the old criminologists the new criminologists have little to say about penology. The failure to mention, or avoidance of mentioning, the subject is almost total, although conceivably some relevant ideas are present as 'unspoken silences', to borrow the curious phrase used by Alvin W. Gouldner in his foreword to the book (p. ix).

The absence of anything more explicit does not seem to be due to reticence so much as to the belief that 'the absence of crime is possible under certain social arrangements' (*ibid.* p. 281). 'The task', we are told, 'is to create a society in which the facts of human diversity, whether personal, organic or social, are not subject to the power to criminalize' (p. 282). The suggestion seems to be that 'under conditions of a free division of labour, untrammelled by the inequalities of inherited wealth and the entrenchment of interests of power and authority (by those who are not deserving of it)' (p. 281), the problems of punishment will not so much be solved as dissolved.

What is required is 'fundamental social change' (p. 282). Those who fail to see this and espouse less radical programmes inevitably become involved in the futilities of 'social welfare oriented criminology', 'reformism' or 'correctionalism' (pp. 280, 281, 301). Thus, 'it should be clear that a criminology which is not normatively committed to the abolition of inequalities of wealth and power, and in particular of inequalities in property and life-chances, is inevitably bound to fall into correctionalism.' It is necessary to 'break entirely with correctionalism' (p. 281).

[1] Ian Taylor, Paul Walton and Jock Young, *The New Criminology: for a Social Theory of Deviance* (London, 1973).

As far as penology in the narrow sense of that word (which refers to prisons and prison management) is concerned, the implication appears to be that the prison is an institution which is the product of 'a society of social arrangements built around the capitalist mode of production' (p. 277). It is necessary to understand the 'political explanation of the necessity to imprison' (p. 279), 'the social and political origins of repression and segregation of deviants' (p. 278).

The most explicit passage on the subject of prisons begins as follows: 'Man is both determined by the fact of his imprisonment, and also determining, in the sense that he creates (and is able to struggle against) his own imprisonment. Some men (the guards) have interests (up to a point) in the maintenance of the imprisonment; others (the inmates, their relatives and sympathizers) do not' (pp. 277–8). Once we understand 'the contingencies and sequences that may lead some men to imprison others' and 'the real political, material and symbolic imperatives that lie at the back of such sequences and processes' we can see that 'man is able consciously to abolish the imprisonment that he consciously created' (p. 278).

What we have here is not a contribution to penology as traditionally conceived. It is rather a political prospectus which carries the implication that what one may call the old penologists with their concern for such matters as prison administration and reforms were guilty of both 'theoretical naïvety and normative incongruity' (p. 301). What they should have been concerned with was 'the social arrangements that have obstructed, and the social contradictions that enhance, man's chances of achieving full sociality—a state of freedom from material necessity, and (therefore) of material incentive, a release from the constraints of forced production, an abolition of the forced division of labour, and a set of social arrangements, therefore, in which there would be no politically, economically, and socially induced need to criminalize deviance' (p. 270).

II The Kropotkin solution

The first thing to be said is that this approach to penology can hardly be described as new. Although the new criminologists do not refer to the fact, a remarkably similar viewpoint is expressed in Peter Kropotkin's *In Russian and French Prisons*.[2] Having spent some five years as a prisoner in a variety of penal institutions Kropotkin was at least as well qualified as most of those who have written on this subject. And like the new criminologists he was in no doubt that prisons should be abolished.

The prison system, he wrote, was 'wrong from the very foundation' (*ibid*. p. 304). There was no point in considering meliorative

[2] Peter Kropotkin, *In Russian and French Prisons* (London, 1887).

measures. There is 'nothing easier than to build adminstration utopias' (p. 332), but 'the more one reflects about the partial improvements which might be made; the more one considers them under their real, practical aspect, the more one is convinced that the few which can be made will be of no moment, while serious improvements are impossible' (pp. 303–4). What was required was a large scale reorganization of society, including 'a thorough transformation of the present relations between work and capital', as a necessary condition of its achievement. 'Some thoroughly new departure is unavoidable' (pp. 365–70).

The new departure Kropotkin had in mind was expounded in terms which although more specific are clearly in the spirit of the new penology. 'Let us organize our society', he wrote, 'so as to assure to everybody the possibility of regular work for the benefit of the commonwealth—and that means, of course, a thorough transformation of the present relations between work and capital; let us assure to every child a sound education and instruction, both in manual labour and science, so as to permit him to acquire, during the first twenty years of his life, the knowledge and habits of earnest work—and we shall be in no more need of dungeons and jails.'

Thus, 'two thirds of all breaches of law being so-called "crimes against property", these cases will disappear, or be limited to a quite trifling amount, when property, which is now the privilege of the few, shall return to its real source—the community.' As for crimes against the person, Kropotkin acknowledged that there would continue to be 'a limited number of persons whose antisocial passions—the result of bodily diseases—may still be a danger to the community'. But to 'lock them up in prisons' would be a 'wicked solution of the difficulty'.

All that was required was 'liberty and fraternal care'. 'Fraternal treatment to check the development of the antisocial feeling which grows up in some of us—not imprisonment—is the only means we are authorized in applying, and can apply, with some effect to those in whom these feelings have developed in consequence of bodily disease or social influences' (p. 353). Unfortunately, Kropotkin did not indulge in further elaboration of the proposed fraternal treatment. The antisocial passions, he said simply, 'can receive another direction, and most of them can be rendered almost or quite harmless by the combined efforts of those who surround us' (p. 367).

The immediate impact of Kropotkin's work must have been diminished by the fact that agents of the Russian government attempted to buy up the entire first edition. They succeeded so well apparently that the author seeking a copy himself shortly afterwards found it unobtainable. However, the book was reissued by another publisher and, according to a somewhat cryptic remark in Kropotkin's biography, 'sufficient precautions were taken this time to prevent a recurrence of the previous incident'.[3] Even so the practical consequences of its publication must have been less than Kropotkin had hoped. Nearly a century later prisons are still with us. Indeed those he condemned still stand and are more than fully occupied. Their number has, in fact, been vastly augmented throughout the world. Prison building programmes continue to be approved and implemented.

Moreover 'the bulky literature of prison discipline' which he despised has also proliferated. Today our library shelves are crowded with a variety of literature on prisons: government publications, historical accounts, reformist tracts, sociological studies, committee investigation reports, the bitter reminiscences of ex-inmates, the ghost-written memoirs of ex-wardens. A great deal of that literature is purely descriptive, although the need for penal reform is a recurrent theme. For the most part, nevertheless, the prison is accepted as a necessary, if not altogether desirable, social institution—'the black flower of our civilization' as Nathaniel Hawthorne described it, but still an essential feature of society.

III This two hundred year old experiment

That is not to say of course that what one may call the Kropotkin solution to the problems of crime and punishment ceased to be canvassed in the years between the publication of *In Russian and French prisons* and the appearance of *The New Criminology*. Thus a notable example of this approach may be found in the writings of Clarence Darrow who declared firmly that 'there should be no jails.... They are a blot upon any civilization'. He argued that there would be no necessity for jails, we could wipe them out if we took the appropriate steps 'to do away with what we call crime'. Moreover he provided a recipe for achieving that objective, although he acknowledged that it was not easy.[4]

'I will tell you how to do it,' he wrote; 'it can be done by giving the people a chance to live—by destroying special privileges.... Make fair conditions of life. Give men a chance to live. Abolish the right of private ownership of land, abolish monopoly, make the world partners in production, partners in the good things of life. Nobody would steal if he could get something of his own some easier way. Nobody will commit burglary when he has a house full. No girl will go out on the streets when she has a comfortable place at home' (*ibid.* pp. 14–15). And so on.

---

[3] George Woodcock and Ivan Avakumović, *The Anarchist Prince* (London and New York, 1950), p. 108.

[4] Clarence S. Darrow, *Crime and Criminals* (1902). Reprinted in *Attorney for the Damned*, edited by Arthur Weinberg (New York, 1957) pp. 14–15.

More recently there has been a widespread revival of this sort of critique with a similar emphasis on the abolition of prisons. And in the writings of those who adopt this position one finds clear echoes of Kropotkin's description of those ' "respectable people" who conceal under a Christian exterior a Pharisaic egotism'; and also of his description of 'the philanthropists who have schemed our prison discipline' as having a 'cold contempt for human nature' (Kropotkin, pp. 319–26). Historians have suggested that the benevolent claims of the designers of the penitentiary really masked hostility to lower-class groups and a desire to provide a dumping ground for social undesirables.[5] Sociologists have argued that the real social function of the prison is to repress deviation from middle-class norms, maintain the status quo and preserve an inequitable social order.

Many penal reformers have abandoned demands for improved prison conditions and adopted as a slogan 'Break Down The Walls'. Imprisonment, it is said, far from being reformative, leads more often to the increased criminalization of those confined. Offenders are more likely to commit further offences when released from prison than if they had been subjected to some alternative punishment. Moreover, what is called 'the rehabilitative ideal' or 'the reformist ideology' or 'the individualized treatment model' is denounced as being in practice more punitive, unjust and inhumane than either the barbarities of earlier centuries or the straightforward pursuit of retribution and deterrence. Prisons are seen as symbols of our hypocrisy regarding rehabilitation, our intolerance of deviants, or our refusal to deal with the root causes of crime such as poverty, discrimination, unemployment, ignorance, overcrowding.

This attitude is well exemplified in *Struggle for Justice*, a report compiled by the American Friends Service Committee's Working Party (which incidentally included Caleb Foote, Professor of Law and Criminology at the University of California at Berkeley and John Irwin, Associate Professor of Sociology at San Francisco State College, both of whom have served terms of imprisonment). In this report the American criminal justice system is condemned as 'an instrument of white Anglo [sic] domination and a barrier to the development of full power within communities of oppressed peoples'.[6] The reader is told a number of times that 'the construction of a just system of criminal justice in an unjust society is a contradiction in terms' (*ibid.* p. 16 and also pp. 13, 99) and warned of the 'impossibility of achieving more than a superficial reformation of our criminal justice system without a radical change in our values and a drastic restructuring of our social and economic institutions' (pp.

[5] David J. Rothman, *The Discovery of the Asylum* (Boston, 1971), *passim*.
[6] *Struggle for Justice: A Report on Crime and Punishment in America*, prepared for the American Friends Service Committee (New York, 1971), p. 112.

12–13). The report is said to be inspired by 'the desire to transfer power from the police/courts/prisons to the people' (p. 171). The truth is that the authors of the report, as they state candidly in their first chapter, 'approach criminal justice from a Quaker perspective' (p. 16), although it cannot be said that this leads them to take a particularly indulgent view of the role played by earlier Quakers in the development of penal reform. In fact they come very close to categorical repudiation in the preface to the report: 'It would be naive not to acknowledge the blunders that an uncritical faith can produce. The horror that is the American prison system grew out of an eighteenth-century reform by Pennsylvania Quakers and others against the cruelty and futility of capital and corporal punishment. This two-hundred-year-old experiment has failed' (p. v).

The authors are extremely critical of the activities of those they label the functionaries of the criminal justice system. 'By and large, the functionaries of a criminal justice system are either members of the politically and economically dominant classes of society or totally subservient to these classes' (p. 39). In so far as those functionaries support the 'treatment-oriented prison reform movement' (p. 85), their attitude is seen as hypocritical and their motives as discreditable.

Thus what is called 'the individualized treatment model' is said to have 'never commanded more than lip service from most of its more powerful adherents' (p. 120). Prison administrators who embraced the rehabilitative ideal are said to have done so because it increased their power over inmates. 'It wasn't treatment that excited them. It was the prospect of having greater control over their prisons' (pp. 85–6). Prison personnel are described as 'unthinking, unfeeling functionaries within institutions' (p. 120).

A major factor in the reform movement is said to have been 'the mixture of hatred, fear and revulsion that white, middle-class Protestant reformers felt toward lower-class persons.... These difficult feelings were disguised as humanitarian concern for the "health" of threatening subculture members. Imprisonment dressed up as treatment was a particularly suitable response for reformers' complicated and inconsistent feelings' (p. 85).

Inevitably this is reflected in prison regimes, so we find that 'as part of treatment and rehabilitation, cultural assimilation is forced upon' offenders. In other words attempts are made by 'officials [who] exaggerate their own importance' and 'the uptight caseworker' to impose 'a middle-class life-style' and 'the increasingly outmoded Protestant work ethic' on them. 'Accepted correctional practice is dominated by indoctrination in white Anglo-Saxon middle-class values' (pp. 43 and 119–20).

The report maintains that 'imprisonment with treatment is identical with traditional imprisonment in most significant aspects' (p. 25). It argues that although 'progressive penology' inspires internal institutional reforms the changes involved are trivial when measured against 'the basic evils of imprisonment'. Imprisonment is criticized as follows: 'It denies autonomy, degrades dignity, impairs or destroys self-reliance, inculcates authoritarian values, minimizes the likelihood of beneficial interaction with one's peers, fractures family ties, destroys the family's economic stability, and prejudices the prisoner's future prospects for any improvement in his economic and social status' (p. 33).

The report makes a number of other specific criticisms of imprisonment although none of them are particularly novel. Thus when the authors complain that 'much that passes for reform is a facade', that 'penal programs are inhibited by bureaucratic and custodial restraints', that 'most institutional employment and training programs are not relevant to the future employment possibilities of the prisoners', and that 'only a minority of those who receive vocational training for some occupation while in prison work at that trade when released' (p. 33), even the slightest familiarity with the literature of penal reform over the past half century will serve to inoculate the reader against any sense of astonishment.

Another writer who agrees with the authors of *Struggle for Justice* is Jessica Mitford. In *Kind and Usual Punishment: The Prison Business* she states that she accepts their contention that without 'a drastic restructuring of our social and economic institutions' anything more than a superficial reformation of the criminal justice system would be impossible.[7] She argues that 'prisons are intrinsically evil and should be abolished' (*ibid.* p. 293). And she quotes approvingly the remark of the federal district judge, James Doyle, of the Western District of Wisconsin who, ruling on a prison censorship case, said of the institution of prison: 'In many respects it is as intolerable within the United States as was the institution of slavery, equally brutalizing to all involved, equally toxic to the social system, equally subversive of the brotherhood of man, even more costly by some standards and probably less rational' (p. 273; also *Morales* v. *Schmidt*, 340 F. Supp. 544, 548–9 [W.D. Wis. 1972], rev'd [7th Cir. 1973]).

Mitford also cites with approval an article by Samuel Jordan writing as an inmate in the Pennsylvania state prison system. Jordan asserts that: 'An inmate or victim is not seeking a more comfortable or more hospitable arrangement with his tormentors. He wants to be completely rid of prisons and those who control them.' He argues that 'in the United States today, prison is a by-product as well as an

[7] Jessica Mitford, *Kind and Usual Punishment: The Prison Business* (New York, 1973), p. 273.

instrument of the class war' and refers to 'the use of the prison as a class weapon.'[8]

IV Practical implications

Now if one asks from the point of view of penology what the practical implications of this sort of critique are the answer is not immediately obvious. In this connection the distinction which Sir Karl Popper draws between 'holistic or utopian social engineering as opposed to piecemeal social engineering' is relevant. For the new penologists are clearly holistic in their approach, in that they aim at the remodelling of the whole of society rather than 'piecemeal tinkering' with particular social institutions or systems, whereas, according to Popper, 'the characteristic approach of the piecemeal engineer is this. Even though he may perhaps cherish some ideals which concern society "as a whole"—its general welfare perhaps—he does not believe in the method of redesigning it as a whole.'[9]

Popper distinguishes between the holistic and piecemeal approaches in terms of the impracticability or unfeasibility of wholesale utopian projects of reform and their incompatibility with a truly scientific attitude. He admits, however, the difficulty of drawing a precise line of demarcation between the two and acknowledges the possibility of ambitious kinds of social engineering such as a whole series of piecemeal reforms inspired by one general tendency.

But in this context the distinction is in effect absolute. The holism of the new penologists does not envisage the transformation of penal institutions but their total dissolution. For the new penologists the lesson of history is that the invention of the penitentiary was quite simply a mistake, or rather a deliberate perversion, and that to pursue the path of amelioration or reform is merely to compound that error. Indeed it may, as Mitford puts it, 'tend to confer legitimacy on the prisons and thus help to perpetuate the system' (Mitford, p. 291). Or, as Samuel Jordan wrote, 'The prison reformer—wittingly or unwittingly—is an agent of capitalism. . . . His mission is to repaint, adjust, or gloss over the flaws in one of society's potent control mechanisms' (Jordan, p. 786).

Not all the new penologists, in fact, take the view that attempts to improve prison conditions must inevitably retard the demise of prisons. Mitford, for example, while acknowledging that 'reforms may strengthen the system in the long run by refurbishing the facade of prison and thus assuaging the public conscience', argues that it is possible to distinguish between two types of reform proposals. There

[8] Samuel Jordan, 'Prison Reform: In Whose Interest?', *Criminal Law Bulletin* 7 (1971), pp. 779–87.
[9] Karl Popper, *The Poverty of Historicism* (2nd edition, London, 1961) pp. 58–70.

are 'those which will result in strengthening the prison bureaucracy, designed to perpetuate and reinforce the system, and those which to one degree or another challenge the whole premise of prison and move in the direction of its eventual abolition'.

Yet it must be said that in view of the way in which all reforms are liable to have unwanted consequences only the gift of prescience would enable anyone to apply this distinction in practice with any degree of success. For it is impossible to know in advance that reforms which are not in the least degree designed to perpetuate and reinforce the system, but are intended merely to make life more tolerable for the prisoner, may not have the unintended consequence of moderating demands for abolition. Thus to take one of Mitford's examples of a reform in the second category, it is by no means certain that proposals aimed 'at restoring to prisoners those constitutional rights that will enable them to organize and fight injustice within the system' (Mitford, pp. 291–3) would, if adopted, tend to accelerate the disintegration of the system. Indeed, it could plausibly be argued that the reverse might be the case.

The authors of *Struggle for Justice* are not much more helpful. Although their criticisms of current practice are trenchant and specific the question of alternatives is dealt with in a curiously opaque fashion. Beyond being advised that we must set about restructuring the entire range of social and economic institutions within our society only desultory suggestions are offered—as, for example, that we must join in 'demonstrating solidarity with prisoners' demands', or that we must set up 'referral services ("manned mostly by young volunteers") directing callers to resources that already exist within the community' (pp. 170–71). For the rest, the authors have a 'vision of a peaceful non-coercive society', in which 'our institutional and non-institutional environments encourage the creation of morally autonomous, self-disciplined people who exercise independent judgment and purpose-fulness from their own inner strength' (p. 45).

There is about the polemics of the new penologists something of the exhilarating character which commonly infects the writing of those who are prepared to follow an argument to its logical conclusion—and beyond. The absence of tiresome qualifications, cautious parentheses and saving clauses seems in itself like a foretaste of the mass liberation proposed. Yet on closer examination it becomes clear that this initial impression is misleading. 'Man', we are told, 'is able to abolish the imprisonment that he consciously created' (Taylor *et al.*, p. 278). Then one finds that the fulfilment of that aim is seen as dependant upon the prior achievement of other changes in social organization, so universal in scope and radical in nature that by comparison the abolition of prisons seems a relatively minor adjustment.

Nor does it seem to be an adjustment which will be rapidly

implemented. Thus Samuel Jordan who 'wants to be completely rid of prisons' and sees them as 'a class weapon' also says that 'weapons or tools of control are not voluntarily discarded by the class in power'. Yet if they are not going to be voluntarily discarded, and if Jordan's description of 'the root of the prison function' as 'the rule of the capitalist agents versus the working class' (Jordan, pp. 779–87) is correct, it must follow that prisons will not be abolished prior to the overthrow of the capitalist system.

The implication is presumably that after that has been accomplished all class weapons will be discarded. But it would require a complete rejection of all the evidence of history to accept that as probable. What seems most likely is that even then 'the abused working-class people' would want to preserve a number of prisons if for no other purpose than to house some of 'the bankers, the chairmen and the bosses' and 'the corporate leaders of the country' or their agents (*ibid.*), who might indulge in counter-revolutionary, or other types of delinquent, activity.

The authors of *Struggle for Justice* appear to recognize some such possibility for while they assert that 'if the choice were between prisons as they are now and no prisons at all, we would promptly choose the latter', they go on to say 'we recognize this is not a real option'. They believe that 'coercive institutions deny our deepest religious and democratic conceptions about the nature and dignity of human beings', but they also say that 'in *some* cases—though we differ on which—most of us accept the necessity of restraining someone against his will and depriving him of his liberty' (*Struggle for Justice*, pp. 23–4; my italics).

Perhaps because of disagreement about whether anyone at all should be deprived of his liberty, and also about who should be imprisoned if the necessity for that measure were agreed on, the Friends' Working Party has little to say about the problems of imprisonment beyond the repetition of largely familiar criticisms of present practice. Indeed apart from benign visions of a peaceful, harmonious society the contributions of all who appear to subscribe to 'the new penology' are so insubstantial as to defy critical analysis.

'The new criminology', one critic has written, 'is more concerned with advocacy than understanding. Specifically, it is concerned with altering the existing system of social arrangements which are said ultimately and inevitably to produce crime. We must produce a new society, or new set of social arrangements, which do not contain within them the seeds of criminality. Unfortunately, we are not told how to do this, nor are we even told whether or not this is possible. Today, we do not even know how to organize a boy scout troop so that there will be no deviance, let alone a society which wishes to eliminate crime.'[10]

[10] Robert F. Meier, review of *The New Criminology* in *Journal of Criminal Justice* 2 (1974), p. 367.

In a world where violence, acquisitiveness, and the pursuit of power show no signs of diminution but rather the reverse, the utopian attitude—for it is an attitude rather than an argument—does constitute, if not a deliberate evasion, at least a fundamental change in perspective in the light of which what others see as urgent, immediate problems are substantially reduced in significance if they are not totally eclipsed. The solution to present problems always seems to be located at some point in space or time removed from the distasteful realities of the world in which we live. Somewhere, sometime, the walls will come down, the morning stars will sing together and all the decarcerated sons of God will shout for joy and become 'morally autonomous, self-disciplined people'; but not here, not now.

V Prospect for penal reform

Rather than attempt to criticize so nebulous a programme, perhaps it will be better in the circumstances to offer a brief assessment of the prospects for penal reform with special reference to the abolition of prisons. This analysis is largely based on the American scene where the penitentiary system originated and where it has reached its fullest development.

It seems reasonable to assume that there will be changes in the size of the prison population or the nature of prisons. It seems likely that we will ultimately come to use the criminal justice system as 'the agency of last resort for social problems' and the prison as 'the last resort for correctional problems'.[11] Certainly the most obvious practical corollaries of past experience are firstly a substantial diminution in the use of imprisonment and further expansion of alternatives to institutionalization; and secondly, the construction of much smaller, specialized custodial establishments designed to meet the diversity of our penal needs and purposes.

But only an extravagantly sanguine reading of the history of penal reform could lead anyone to anticipate rapid progress along these lines. In 1954 Thorsten Sellin writing about American prisons said: 'Twenty-three years ago . . . riots and disturbances had revealed glaring defects in our prison system. Most of those defects still exist for progress in penology moves on leaden feet.'[12]

Two decades later Sellin would need to change only a few words. Two decades later, Hans W. Mattick, after twenty years working in the field of criminal justice, formulated his 'pessimistic hypothesis'. Periodically, he wrote, there is in this field 'criticism, exposure and

[11] US National Advisory Commission on Criminal Justice Standards and Goals, *Task Force Report: Corrections* (Washington, D.C., 1973), p. 2.
[12] Thorsten Sellin, foreword to *Annals of the American Academy of Political and Social Science* 293 (1954), p. vii.

crisis. . . . When that happens the routine response of the larger society, through its political representatives, is to enact a ritual known as "fixing the responsibility".' But the main purpose this ritual serves is 'to buy the time necessary to mollify a transiently aroused public interest. . . . The tumult and shouting dies. . . . The real captains and kings do not depart. The more things seem to change, the more they remain the same. . . . The stage is set for a later repetition of the same cycle.'[13]

There is no doubt that Mattick is right about the cyclical pattern he identifies. Part of the reason for its persistence is probably the fact that what Daniel Bell calls 'Tocqueville's law' does not directly apply to prisoners. Tocqueville's law states that 'in a society pledged to the idea of equality, what the few have today, the many will demand tomorrow.' Insofar as this is true, it is possible to make certain kinds of predictions about social trends by reference to the kinds of demands that will be made by disadvantaged groups. Bell cites the history of trade unionism by way of example and the way in which privileges once held by the managerial and white-collar class—pensions and security—later became diffused throughout the blue-collar class. Thus, 'one can chart similar rates of diffusion for the civil rights movement, for medical care for the population, for higher education for the greater proportion of youths and so forth.'[14]

Prisons are not wholly excluded from this process of diffusion. But powerful constraints on change operate in their case which not only impede progress in penology but render prediction in this sphere more than usually problematic. One of these constraints is the prisoners' lack of any political leverage. Another is the operation of the principle of less eligibility which derives from Jeremy Bentham and in this context requires that the condition of the prisoner should be inferior, or at least not superior, to that of the lowest classes of the non-criminal population in a state of liberty. There is no doubt that this principle, which underlies much of the common thinking about the treatment of criminals, has always constituted a formidable barrier to penal reform. And it is surely utterly illusory to anticipate that in this field there is any likelihood that we shall move rapidly forward. Progressive politicians and correctional administrators who assume that penal reform is widely accepted as 'a good thing' which reasonable people everywhere will automatically endorse are no more realistic than those whose distaste for the twentieth century induces them to keep their gaze fixed yearningly backwards.

In America in 1971, after the Attica uprising, Professor Herman Schwartz said: 'I hope that people will realize, apart from the killing of hostages, that what happened at Attica was the inevitable result of the

---

[13] Hans W. Mattick, 'The Pessimistic Hypothesis', *Public Welfare* 31 (1973), pp. 2–5.
[14] Daniel Bell (ed.), *Toward the Year 2000* (Boston, 1968), p. 328.

inhumanity that man perpetrates against his fellow men in the name of justice.' Norman Carlson, Director of the US Federal Bureau of Prisons, said: 'I am even more convinced that the long-run effect of Attica will be a positive step forward for prison reform.' Linda Singer of the Center for Correctional Justice said: 'Attica has alerted people to the fact that we are running a very repressive, self-defeating correction system. More and more people are becoming aware that the system not only is unhumane, but dysfunctional from the point of view of public safety, economics, or almost any way you want to look at it.'[15]

It may appear cynical four years later to ask how large a step forward for prison reform was accomplished at that time. It may seem captious to enquire to what extent the general public in America does realize that the prison system is repressive, self-defeating, inhumane and dysfunctional. But it is surely to the point to ask how many of America's great maximum security prisons—'these big Bastilles' as Dr Preston Sharp of the American Correctional Association called them—have been shut down in the years since Attica. The answer of course is—not one.

Today roughly half of the approximately 100,000 felons in maximum security facilities in the United States are still housed in prisons built prior to 1900. Twenty-six such prisons each contain well over 1,000 inmates, the largest holding nearly 4,000; and one third of them are overcrowded. The oldest, Virginia Penitentiary, was erected in 1797; and its ancient cellblocks, too, are currently overcrowded. At the time they were built, some of them were among the most costly buildings the world had seen since the Pyramids, although intended to house the living rather than the dead. Like the Pyramids, they were built to endure and they have endured. Despite increasingly lethal explosions of violence within and persistent and mounting critical assaults from without, they still dominate the correctional landscape throughout the world, not merely picturesque monuments but living institutions, seemingly almost imperishable, both impregnable to attack and immune to the ravages of time.

Moreover, since 1900 the Americans have built 27 new state and federal prisons with room for more than 1,000 prisoners apiece (most recently at Lucasville, Ohio in 1972); and nearly half of them are overcrowded. The state prison of Southern Michigan holds the distinction of heading the list with a capacity for 4,764 inmates, and in the 1950s held more than 6,000 prisoners. These institutions, as the US National Advisory Commission on Criminal Justice Standards and Goals stated, 'form the backbone of our present-day correctional system'. There is no indication that there has been any significant change in attitude on the part of those in positions of responsibility in

[15] Herman Schwartz, 'Attica: A look at the Causes and the Future', *Criminal Law Bulletin* 7 (1971), p. 822. Norman Carlson, *ibid.* p. 832. Linda Singer, *ibid.* p. 841.

the correctional systems of America. It is not merely that the present prisons are seen as necessary; plans for new prisons have been approved and are in the process of implementation.

To give only one example, in May 1972 the relatively enlightened Federal Bureau of Prisons, ignoring the recommendations of several national advisory commissions (for a moratorium on prison construction), published its 'long range master plan'. One critic, William G. Nagel, Director of the American Foundation Incorporated, Institute of Corrections, commented on the master plan: 'A bureaucracy which had existed with only three prisons during its first thirty years, and which had gradually increased to 24 facilities during its next four decades suddenly now planned to add 35 new correctional institutions costing over 500 million dollars. During a decade when people all over the country were seriously questioning— even rejecting—the desirability of creating any new correctional institutions at all the Federal Bureau decided to go construction crazy.'[16]

Another consideration which leads to the conclusion that the use of imprisonment as a punishment will be regarded as necessary for some time to come derives from the analyses of society's use of punishment to be found in the work of Nils Christie and Alfred Blumstein and Jacqueline Cohen.[17] What emerges from both these articles, the first dealing with Scandinavian data and the second principally with the US data, is the constancy of the imprisonment rate over long periods of time. Thus Christie demonstrates a remarkable stability in the imprisonment rates for Norway for the period 1880 to 1964 and a very similar pattern in Denmark and Sweden. Blumstein and Cohen show that, at a much higher level, the stability of the imprisonment rate in the United States for the period 1930–70 was even more striking. It is of course not possible on the basis of the evidence provided to accept unreservedly the 'conservation theory that suggests that society tries to impose a fairly constant level of punishment' (Blumstein and Cohen, p. 207). But there is certainly nothing to suggest that the institution of imprisonment is likely to be regarded as dispensable in the imminent future.

According to Thorsten Sellin the origins of imprisonment are lost in antiquity. It has proved to be the most perdurable of all penal methods, despite all the premature obituary notices. It is not impossible that eventually the maximum security prison as we know it will be replaced

[16] William G. Nagel, 'An American Archipelago: The Federal Bureau of Prisons', address to the National Institute on Crime and Delinquency (1974), p.6.

[17] Nils Christie, 'Changes in Penal Values' in N. Christie (ed.), *Aspects of Social Control in Welfare States*, Scandinavian Studies in Criminology 2 (Oslo, 1968), pp. 161–72. Alfred Blumstein and Jacqueline Cohen, 'A Theory of the Stability of Punishment', *Journal of Criminal Law and Criminology* 64 (1973), pp. 198–207.

by 'small non-punitive custodial treatment centres, psychiatrically and/or sociologically based, and adapted to individual needs'.[18] But it is surely both a perverse denial of experience and irresponsible to abjure attempts to deal with present problems because of the prospect of an imagined futurity.

Over half a century ago Sidney and Beatrice Webb wrote, at the conclusion of their survey of English prison history: 'The reflection emerges that, when all is said and done, it is probably impossible to make a good job of the deliberate incarceration of human beings in the most enlightened of dungeons. . . . We suspect that it passes the wit of man to contrive a prison which shall not be gravely injurious to the minds of the vast majority of the prisoners, if not also to their bodies. So far as can be seen at present, the most hopeful of "prison reforms" is to keep people out of prison altogether.' Moreover they reported progress 'in this direction . . . during the last two decades.'[19] But, although the Webbs were founders of the Fabian Society, it seems likely that the interminable protraction of that progress would, were they still alive, have exceeded even their predilection for gradualness and their preference for slow rather than revolutionary change. For the truth is that the incarceration rate in England and Wales is actually higher than it was a century ago.[20]

Prisons have survived in part because of what Morris and Zimring once referred to as 'the four horsemen of political inaction: inertia, irresponsibility, ignorance and cost'.[21] But other factors have also been in operation to preserve them—fear, resentment, vengefulness and even, although it is fashionable to forget or depreciate them, idealism and compassion. Their roots lie deep in the nature of man and human society and will tenaciously resist extirpation. To recognize this is not pessimism but realism; to refuse to recognize it is an evasion which can only tend to increase the amount of human suffering and waste involved in imprisonment.

VI Afterword on Attica

A final topic is relevant here. This concerns the question to what extent there have been in recent years significant changes in the demands and attitudes of prisoners themselves which may force the

[18] Giles Playfair and Derrick Sington, *Crime, Punishment and Cure* (London, 1965), p. 336.

[19] Sidney and Beatrice Webb, *English Prisons under Local Government* (London and New York, 1922), pp. 247–8.

[20] Leslie T. Wilkins, 'Directions for Corrections', *Proceedings of the American Philosophical Society* 118 (1974), p. 236.

[21] Norval Morris and Franklin E. Zimring, 'Deterrence and Corrections', *Annals of the American Academy of Political and Social Science* 381 (1969), p. 138.

adoption of some kind of new penology by the correctional authorities. For clearly if it were true that a substantial majority of prison inmates subscribed to the revolutionary or radical ideology which underlies the new penology this would have important implications for penal policy.

In fact, however, the evidence suggests that the notion that there has been any widespread radicalization of prison populations or that among prisoners generally there is any marked solidarity or community of attitude in opposition to 'the system' seems principally to be the product of impressionistic interpretation rather than objective, empirical research.

Objective studies paint a rather different picture. Thus Stanton Wheeler's work indicates that some of the conflict between prisoners and the authorities is more apparent than real, and that there is much less genuine conflict between inmates and staff than has been commonly assumed on the basis of unsystematic observation.[22] In the same vein, but rather more positively, Glaser reports: 'Our findings from several different types of inquiry indicated that inmates *have a predominant interest in adjusting to the demands of the institution and that they have strong non-criminal aspirations.* However, evidence and deductive reasoning supported the notion that inmates and others generally overestimate the extent of inmate opposition to staff-supported standards, because inmates who oppose these standards are most articulate'.[23]

It is interesting to note that Emery's study of an English prison lays considerable stress on the fact that insofar as both custodial officers and inmates 'come as adult men from the same society, they bring into the prison certain common values and standards [which] . . . even if they do not carry much weight in any particular instance, do have the character of persistent, impersonal psychological forces'.[24] Emery makes the significant point that 'unless there were such strongly held common values, one suspects that inmates and staff alike would be very much less sensitive to the implicit, and sometimes explicit, criticism they make of each other'.

More specifically he reports that 'social values specifying the immorality of a crime seem to be commonly held both by officers and inmates. Despite the theoretical speculations about "criminal cultures", which divorce crime of any moral significance, there was little evidence in this case to suggest that inmates regarded their crimes as anything other than immoral.' He goes on to point out that 'criminal

[22] Stanton Wheeler, 'Role Conflict in Correctional Communities' in Donald R. Cressey (ed.), *The Prison: Studies in Institutional Organization and Change* (New York, 1961), p. 230.

[23] Daniel Glaser, *The Effectiveness of a Prison and Parole System* (Indianapolis, 1964), p. 118.

[24] Fred E. Emery, *Freedom and Justice Within Walls* (London and New York, 1970), p. 33.

offences that are socially regarded as being most immoral, e.g., sexual offences against minors, are similarly regarded by officers and prisoners. . . . Other offences which carry little moral significance in the outside world, particularly among the working classes (brawling, drunkenness, motoring offences) are found to be equally free from moral condemnation among staff and prisoners.'

It might be argued of course that in United States prisons the existence of such common or complementary values is less common and that even where it did once exist the 'radicalization' of the prison population has produced a situation in which prisoners everywhere are boldly challenging conventional bourgeois morality and are refusing to accept the personal devaluation involved in acknowledging that they have done anything wrong. But although there is clearly an element of truth in this assertion it is questionable first, whether what is happening, or has happened, represents any very novel development and second, to what extent it is a genuinely revolutionary movement.

As to the first question, there have always been prisoners whose defence against their rejection and devaluation has taken the form of a challenge to established morality. Even in the English situation, Emery describes inmates whose self-justification in the face of the moral charge against them 'is essentially that, while they have done wrong and probably intend to go on doing wrong, this is not simply because they lack these values but because they attach greater importance to other human values. In particular, they would claim to lay great value on individual autonomy, that is, the fulfilment of individual desires in the face of a hostile and unrewarding environment, (*ibid.* pp. 33–5). This kind of defensive self-evaluation is not very far removed from, and is indeed frequently linked with, an offensive devaluation not only of law-abiding members of society but also of society itself.

As to the second question, a concrete example may help to put the matter in perspective. On 27 September 1971 *Time* magazine ran a cover story on the Attica uprising ('War at Attica') which was in many ways an admirable exercise in vivid news reporting. In the story some reference was made to the demands which were formulated by the Attica prisoners. They were described as 'revolutionary'. *Time* was not alone in this characterization because throughout the media those demands were cited as demonstrating the prisoners' dangerous radicalism. Indeed this interpretation of the events at Attica was and still is widely supported.

Angela Davis wrote: 'Attica before the massacre offered us a sleeping but graphic glimpse of the monumental feats obtainable by men and women moving along a revolutionary course. . . . In a figurative sense, it evoked visions of the Paris Communes, the liberated areas of prerevolutionary Cuba, the free territories of

Mozambique.[25] and Russell G. Oswald, New York Commissioner of Corrections, has also warned that the troublesome prisoners were revolutionaries and that the attack on prisons was the first step in a broader assault on society. In his *Attica: My Story* he speaks of 'leftist militants . . . who . . . seek to turn America's correctional system into a revolutionary battle ground'.[26] And again, 'On the eve of Attica, then, the disinherited and the villainous, the alienated and the pawns, the flotsam and jetsam of society, and a new generation of revolutionary leaders focused on the prisons as their point of leverage. Here was where the Establishment could be made to buckle and the class issue could be most clearly defined' (*ibid.* p. 12).

It is instructive by way of contrast with the rhetoric to look at the 'Immediate demands' and the 'practical proposals' put forward by the Attica inmates. Apart from those which arose specifically out of the riot situation, such as the requests for an amnesty for inmates taking part in the rebellion, the sacking of the warden, and transportation to a non-imperialist country (which was soon dropped) the list is remarkably innocuous. Most of it could easily have been compiled by a group of white Anglo-Saxon middle-class Protestant prison reformers. They requested 'realistic, effective rehabilitation programs for all inmates according to their offence and personal needs'.[27] They asked for a variety of things such as modernized inmate educational system, expanded work-release programmes, adequate medical treatment, the abolition of censorship of newspapers, magazines and other publications, freedom for inmates (at their own expense) to communicate with anyone they please.

It is difficult to see why any of these items should be regarded as revolutionary. None of them constituted a rejection of, or a threat to, the system. Professor Herman Schwartz of the State University of New York at Buffalo, who took part in negotiations with the Attica prisoners, spoke of them as a very limited set of demands leaving out 'a lot of things that would be put in if you were going to have complete penal reform'. Nor did Commissioner Oswald regard them, at that time, as especially subversive. In fact we are told: 'Schwartz recalls that Oswald responded to each proposal, and told the inmates he agreed "in principle" with most of them.'[28] There can have been little difficulty for him in this since most of the proposals were things he had earlier promised to implement given more time.

[25] Angela Y. Davis, 'Lessons: From Attica to Soledad', *New York Times*, 8 October, 1971, p. 43.

[26] Russell G. Oswald, *Attica: My Story* (Garden City, N.Y., 1972), p. vii.

[27] Herman Badillo and Milton Haynes, *A Bill of No Rights: Attica and the American Prison System* (New York, 1972), p. 56.

[28] *Attica: The Official Report of the New York State Special Commission on Attica* (New York, 1972), p. 223.

There is a derisive remark near the end of *Struggle For Justice* which is directed at conventional penologists. 'The experts', says the report, '—even the most enlightened and progressive—also line up solidly in support of the system asking only for more of the same' (p. 156). Yet if we read carefully the Attica prisoner proposals, the conclusion is inescapable that that is precisely what the prisoners too were doing— asking for more of the same. Their demands do not constitute a revolutionary manifesto or even an assault on the foundations of the institution of imprisonment. There is little in them which does not fully accord with the spirit of the celebrated 'Declaration of Principles' adopted by the first American National Prison Congress held at Cincinnati in 1870.

Nor did the prisoners behave like revolutionaries. When one looks at the riots in American prisons in recent years their most surprising feature is that the prisoners have exercised appreciable restraint in their revolts. Even those who feel no sympathy for them whatsoever must acknowledge the factual point that they have in their riots and violence stopped far short of inflicting those deaths and injuries on prison staff which it was certainly in their power to encompass. Indeed it could be said that the real tragedy of Attica is that at issue in that confrontation, in which 43 men died (a death toll surpassed only once before in the history of American prison riots), was really only the simple request that we implement promises over a century old that have not been kept.

Even at Attica, as the New York State Special Commission discovered, the impression that the administration was confronted with a solid mass of implacably hostile inmates was quite false. Indeed one prisoner whose testimony has the ring of truth to it told the Commission: 'Well, I think the actual expectations, what individual inmates wanted, varied. There were guys in there that all they wanted was more pink ice cream, we will say, and there were guys in there that were concerned about getting cake in the mess hall and there were guys that were deeply concerned about improving the parole system and trying to get fresh minds into the institution; to do something about rehabilitation. I got the impression myself that there wasn't any real consensus between any more than 50 people. I don't think you could have gotten 50 people that could have agreed on any one point' (*Attica: The Official Report*, p. 206).

It is somewhat ironic that while the new penologists are vigorously repudiating the rehabilitative ideal some of the most active of the 'radical' prisoners, on whose behalf this rejection is, theoretically, proposed, should have, in their published proposals at any rate, forcefully endorsed it. Clearly this has implications for penal policy, but hardly in the direction of the new penology.

Certainly in the climate of ferocious sansculottism portrayed by

Angela Davis and Commissioner Russell Oswald, rehabilitative programmes could only appear as quaint academic or administrative aberrations. But they take on a rather different complexion in the light of the Attica prisoners' own demands for 'realistic rehabilitation programs for all inmates' (Badillo and Haynes, p. 56).

Contributors

Robert Brown is Professorial Fellow in the History of Ideas in the Institute of Advanced Studies of the Australian National University, editor of the *Australasian Journal of Philosophy*, and a fellow and executive member of the Academy of the Social Sciences in Australia. Born in New York in 1920, he was educated there at the McBurney School and then at the University of New Mexico, the University of Chicago and University College, London, where he took his doctorate in 1952. He has lectured at universities in California, Wisconsin, and Massachusetts. He is the author of *Explanation in Social Science* (1963) and *Rules and Laws in Sociology* (1973), the editor of *Between Hume and Mill* (1970), and the co-editor of *Contemporary Philosophy in Australia* (1969). Besides publishing extensively in philosophical journals in North America, Britain and Australia, he has contributed to *Explanation in the Behavioral Sciences*, edited by R. Borger and F. Cioffi (1970), and to *Rationality in the Social Sciences*, edited by S. I. Benn and G. Mortimore (1976). At present he is working on a history of the idea of social laws.

Gordon Hawkins is Associate Professor in Criminology in the University of Sydney, and a member of the Australian Law Reform Commission. Born in 1919, he was educated at University College, Cardiff and Balliol College, Oxford. He saw service in the Second World War in North Africa, Italy and Burma, and became police officer and magistrate in Assam in 1945–6. Later he was an assistant prison governor in the UK, a research fellow in the University of Wales and assistant principal of the Prison Staff College at Wakefield, before coming to the University of Sydney Law School in 1961. He has for a number of years also been research fellow at the Center for Studies in Criminal Justice at the University of Chicago. He is the author of *The Prison: Policy and*

Practice (1976) and *Beyond Reasonable Doubt* (1977) and co-author with Norval Morris of *The Honest Politician's Guide to Crime Control* (1970) and *Letter to the President on Crime Control* (1977) and with F. E. Zimring of *Deterrence: The Legal Threat in Crime Control* (1973). His articles range over problems of deterrence, treatment of violent criminals and sexual offenders, pornography, homosexuality, abortion and reform of the criminal law.

Eugene Kamenka is Foundation Professor in the History of Ideas in the Institute of Advanced Studies of the Australian National University and has been (in 1973, 1974 and 1976) Visiting Professor in the Faculty of Law in the University of Sydney. He is a fellow of the Academy of the Social Sciences in Australia and fellow and secretary of the Australian Academy of the Humanities. Born in Cologne, Germany, in 1928, Professor Kamenka was educated in Australia in the Sydney Technical High School, Sydney University and the Australian National University. He has worked and taught in Israel, England, Germany, the United States, Canada and Singapore, and has spent a year as visiting research worker in the Faculty of Philosophy in the Moscow State University. His books include *The Ethical Foundations of Marxism* (1962), *Marxism and Ethics* (1969) and *The Philosophy of Ludwig Feuerbach* (1970); he has edited *A World in Revolution?* (1970) *Paradigm for Revolution? The Paris Commune 1871–1971* (1972), *Nationalism—The Nature and Evolution of an Idea* (1973) and—with R. S. Neale—*Feudalism, Capitalism and Beyond* (1975). He is general editor of this series, 'Ideas and Ideologies'.

William L. Morison is Professor of Law in the University of Sydney. Born in 1920, he was educated at North Sydney Boys' High School, the University of Sydney and Canberra University College. He took his doctorate at Oxford University in 1951 and was a post-doctoral student at Yale Law School in three subsequent years. He has held fellowships at Yale and the Australian National Univeristy and in 1975 was elected a fellow of the World Academy of Art and Science. He trained as a solicitor and is a member of the New South Wales Law Reform Commission and subsequently reported on the reform of the law of privacy under commission from the Australian Commonwealth and State Attorneys General. His recent publications include 'Myres S. McDougal and Twentieth-Century Jurisprudence', comprising chapter 1 of *Toward World Order and Human Dignity*, edited by W. M. Reisman and B. H. Weston (1976). He has also published articles in law journals in England, the United States, Canada and Australia on matters of legal theory and law.

Alice Erh-Soon Tay is Professor of Jurisprudence in the University of Sydney. She was born in Singapore in 1934 and educated at Raffles Girls' School, Singapore, Lincoln's Inn and the Australian National University, where she took her doctorate with a thesis on 'The Concept of Possession in the Common Law'. She has practised in criminal law and lectured in law in the (then) University of Malaya in Singapore and the Australian National University, spent 1965–6 and part of 1973 as a visiting research worker in the Faculty of Law in Moscow State University and been senior fellow at the Russian Institute and the Research Institute on Communist Affairs of Columbia University, New York, and in the East-West Center of the University of Hawaii. She is the author of numerous articles on common law, jurisprudence, comparative law, Soviet law and Chinese law, and of several contributions to the *Encyclopedia of Soviet Law*, besides being co-author, with her husband, Eugene Kamenka, of a forthcoming book, *Marxism and the Theory of Law*. She is an executive member of the International Association for Philosophy of Law and Social Philosophy and served as president of the Association's 1977 World Congress held in Sydney and Canberra.

Index